S0-ARX-816

# REFERRING

# International Library of Philosophy and Scientific Method

EDITOR: TED HONDERICH
ADVISORY EDITOR: BERNARD WILLIAMS

A Catalogue of books already published in the
*International Library of Philosophy and Scientific Method*
will be found at the end of this volume.

# REFERRING

by

Leonard Linsky

LONDON
## ROUTLEDGE & KEGAN PAUL
NEW YORK : HUMANITIES PRESS

*First published 1967*
*by Routledge & Kegan Paul Limited*
*Broadway House, 68–74 Carter Lane*
*London, EC4V 5EL*

*Reprinted 1969*
*Reprinted 1973*

*Printed in Great Britain by*
*Redwood Press Limited*
*Trowbridge, Wiltshire*

*Copyright Leonard Linsky 1967*

*No part of this book may be reproduced*
*in any form without permission from*
*the publisher, except for the quotation*
*of brief passages in criticism*

*ISBN 0 7100 3636 1*

3
340
.55

# CONTENTS

'. . . that paradigm of philosophy,
Russell's theory of descriptions.'

F. P. RAMSEY

# PREFACE

The topic of referring has had a central position in philosophical discussion from the very beginning of this century. Russell was concerned with it in his *Principles of Mathematics* of 1903. At about the same time both Frege and Meinong were developing views on the subject. In 1905 Russell rejected his earlier theory as well as the theories of Frege and Meinong as he understood them. In this year he published 'On Denoting', presenting his famous Theory of Descriptions. Russell was convinced in 1905 that his new theory provided definitive solutions for all of the problems '. . . which a theory as to denoting ought to be able to solve . . .'[1] Russell is notorious for his propensity to change his mind about his earlier views, but he has never abandoned the claims he put forward in 1905 on behalf of his Theory of Descriptions.

It is difficult to exaggerate the prestige which Russell's work on this subject attained. In the forty-five years preceding the publication of Strawson's 'On Referring'[2], Russell's theory was practically immune from criticism. There is not a similar phenomenon in contemporary philosophy. One unfortunate consequence was that the views of those whom Russell had criticized on this topic fell into nearly complete oblivion. Since Russell had solved the problems, it was not necessary to examine the alternative views of Frege and Meinong. Frege's great essay, 'On Sense and Reference', was not translated into English until 1949, nearly sixty years after it was written. The first English translation of Meinong's subtle work had to wait until 1960. In American and English philosophy to be untranslated is to be ignored.

Since 1950 there has been an active controversy between those who accept Strawson's criticisms of Russell and the defenders of

---

[1] 'On Denoting', *Mind*, 1905, reprinted in *Logic and Knowledge*, by Bertrand Russell, Allen and Unwin, London, 1956, pp. 41–56.
[2] 'On Referring', *Mind*, 1950, reprinted in *Essays in Conceptual Analysis*, edited by A. G. N. Flew, Macmillan Co., London, 1956.

Russell. The topic of referring has become a test case in a conflict of opposing schools of philosophical analysis. I hope to accomplish several objectives in this essay. I wish to present an accurate account of some of the relevant views of Meinong and Frege. It seems to me that in some respects their theories are superior to Russell's. But I am also concerned to show where these theories are mistaken, weak, or inadequate.

Famous as Russell's theory is, there does not exist a detailed, critical exposition of it. I have tried to present a complete account of the theory and of Russell's reasons for accepting it. One thing which emerges from this account is that Russell's Theory of Descriptions involves doctrines in epistemology, metaphysics, logic, as well as the philosophy of language. Some of what Russell says is true and some of it not. Some of it is unintelligible. I have done my best to sort these things out.

Another of my objectives is to evaluate the Russell–Strawson controversy; to decide who is right and who is wrong on which points and why. But I have not been concerned exclusively with the views of others. Where these views have seemed right to me I have said so. Where they seem wrong I have also said so; and I have always tried both to prove, in these cases, that they are wrong and to say what is right. This essay contains my own contributions (where those of others have seemed inadequate) towards the solutions of the problems with which it deals.

There is a happy custom of acknowledging one's debts to others in a preface. My greatest debt, of course, is to Lord Russell. This work would not have come into existence had not his work preceded it. I cannot accept all that he says, but I accept Ramsey's view that Russell's Theory of Descriptions is (and ought to be) a paradigm of philosophy. (*A* paradigm, not *the* paradigm—nothing can be that.) The philosophical theory which is beyond criticism has not and will not be produced. To criticize is not to disparage, nor is criticism incompatible with respect. At any rate, I do not believe that the time will ever come when Russell's views on the topics of this essay will deserve to be ignored.

Closer to home I owe a debt of gratitude to my colleagues and friends. Norman Kretzmann and Charles Caton first suggested to me that I undertake the present work. I am grateful to them for that. Many persons at the University of Illinois have helped to clarify my ideas and to correct mistakes. I am indebted to Robert

Swartz, Bruce Goldberg, Ruth Barcan Marcus, and especially to Charles Caton. I wish to thank Sylvain Bromberger, who attended my seminar at the University of Chicago in 1964, for his valuable criticism and encouragement. I had the advantage of many fruitful discussions with Elizabeth Anscombe and John Dolan during my second visit to the University of Chicago in 1965. I am grateful to Bernard Williams and to Ted Honderich for comments which helped to clarify the text at several points; to Glenna Wilson for typing and retyping portions of the final draft during the last year and a half; to Joseph Agassi for his unfailing encouragement and good advice.

It remains to say a word about the audience to whom my work is addressed. My readers are supposed to have some knowledge of elementary logic, but no more than can be acquired in a short time with the aid of a standard modern introductory text. Beyond this I have not relied upon any special background of preparation on the part of the reader. My aim has been to make the book self-contained; to include within it whatever is needed to follow and appreciate its arguments. Therefore, before entering upon criticism or development of the views of other philosophers, I have expounded the relevant doctrines. But exposition has been kept to the minimum required for self-containment. Whatever value the work has must lie in its original contributions.

LEONARD LINSKY

*Florence,*
*August, 1966*

'. . . in this chapter we shall consider the word *the* in the singular, and in the next chapter we shall consider the word *the* in the plural. It may be thought excessive to devote two chapters to one word, but to the philosophical mathematician it is a word of very great importance; like Browning's Grammarian with the enclitic δε, I would give the doctrine of this word if I were 'dead from the waist down' and not merely in prison.'

BERTRAND RUSSELL
*Introduction to Mathematical Philosophy*

# INTRODUCTION

This essay is a study of philosophical problems associated with the concepts of referring, denoting, naming. But the centre of gravity of the work is Russell's Theory of Descriptions. What is said in each of the following chapters is related in one way or another to doctrines of Russell's which are included under the name 'The Theory of Descriptions'. In a sense, then, my essay is an examination of Russell's theory.

Chapter I presents the problems. They are all stated in Russell's 'On Denoting' of 1905, but they are much older than that paper. Two of Russell's great predecessors, Meinong and Frege, were much concerned with them. Indeed, some of these problems appear in the dialogues of Plato. So in this chapter they are presented not only in the form they took for Russell but also as they arose for Meinong, Frege, and others.

In the second chapter I deal with Meinong's theory of objects and in the third with Frege's theory of sense and reference. Meinong's theory attempts to solve one of the problems about referring which is presented in the first chapter. Meinong's work was known to Russell, and Russell admired Meinong as a thinker of great subtlety. But he misunderstood him. He thought that the main achievement of his own theory was that it provided an acceptable alternative to what he regarded as the excesses of Meinong. Russell came to view Meinong as a philosopher who, in face of philosophical difficulties, had abandoned his sense of reality. Meinong, according to Russell, believed in chimeras, unicorns, even the round square. 'In such theories, it seems to me,' he says, 'there is a failure of that feeling for reality which ought to be preserved even in the most abstract studies. Logic, I should maintain, must no more admit a unicorn than zoology can; for logic is concerned with the real world just as truly as zoology, though with its more abstract and general features.'[1]

[1] *Introduction to Mathematical Philosophy*, 2nd edn., Allen and Unwin, London, 1920, p. 169.

I believe that Russell's Meinong is not the real Meinong. There is, however, a philosopher who really did hold the doctrines which Russell attributes to Meinong, viz., Russell himself in his *Principles of Mathematics* of 1903.

In Chapter III I present the other theory which Russell regarded as an alternative to his own, Frege's. I show how Frege deals with the problems of the first chapter and I consider Russell's reasons for rejecting Frege's solutions. As he misunderstood Meinong, so Russell also misunderstood Frege. This latter fact, unlike the former, is now widely acknowledged. But from the fact that Russell rejected the views of his predecessors for the wrong reasons, it does not follow either that those theories are right or that his own theory is inadequate.

Chapter IV contains an exposition of Russell's Theory of Descriptions. The reasons he urged in support of the theory are analysed and criticized. His underlying assumptions are uncovered. Here we deal with doctrines which have been among the most important and influential in philosophy during this century. The phrase 'the theory of descriptions' is not itself a 'proper' description. It does not refer to just one doctrine but to a number of doctrines. 'The Theory of Descriptions' is a name for a collection of views; some of them logical, some epistemological, some semantical, and some ontological. Beside being all of these things, Russell's treatment of his problems involves a certain view as to the task of philosophical analysis and a view as to how to proceed in doing philosophy. As we shall see, these views are also at issue in the discussions of Russell's work.

The contention of Chapter V is that Russell completely failed to provide a satisfactory solution for one of the problems he designed his theory to solve. Here we are concerned with difficulties which arise for the Russellian analysis when one confronts the so-called 'propositional attitudes' and 'non-extensional' contents. Not only is the name 'The Theory of Descriptions' a name for a host of doctrines but the claims which Russell made for the theory changed between 1905, when it was first put forth, and 1910, when the first edition of *Principia* was published. They changed specifically with regard to problems of non-extensionality, and in Chapter V I show why.

The most serious and sustained criticism to which Russell's theory has been subjected is to be found in Strawson's famous 'On

Referring'. 'On Referring' is a landmark in contemporary philosophy and among the most important papers published in philosophy in our time. To confirm this judgment one has only to open contemporary journals and books and to notice how often references are made to it; how frequently it is reprinted; how often it is attacked and defended. It is doubtful that any other philosophical essay published in this century has received more attention, though a plausible candidate is Russell's 'On Denoting'. A principal objective of Strawson's paper is to refute Russell's Theory of Descriptions. Russell's theory had attained the status which F. P. Ramsey said it had. He said it was 'a paradigm of philosophy'. The importance of Strawson's essay derives, in part, from the fact that it rejects this paradigm. Further, in the view of many it has become itself a new paradigm to replace the older one. So the topic of referring has, to a certain extent, become a battlefield, where what seems to be at stake is a decision between alternative ways of doing philosophy. Russell's Theory of Descriptions was not subjected to serious criticism until nearly fifty years after it was put forth. When the criticism came, it came as part of a change in philosophy itself, a change so great that to some it seemed 'a revolution in philosophy'. In the sixth chapter of this work I attempt to draw a balance sheet of the controversy, decide where Russell was right and where Strawson. The chapter contains an exposition of Strawson's views and a criticism of his criticisms. My general conclusion is that, however excellent Strawson's work is on other grounds, it largely fails as an attack on Russell.

Chapter VII deals with some of the views of W. V. Quine on the topics of this essay. There is much which he says which repeats, in other terms, the views of Frege. The main difference, perhaps, is that motivated by extensionalist scruples he attempts to dispense with Frege's indirect reference. Instead of names having an indirect reference in certain anomalous contexts as they do for Frege, Quine regards names in such contexts as not having any reference at all—or at least not having 'pure reference' to their objects. Quine also dispenses with Russell's distinction between proper names and descriptive phrases in dealing with these problems. Instead, his discussion is carried on in terms of an undifferentiated category of 'singular terms'. If my analysis is correct, Quine has ignored these distinctions or some substitute for them at his peril.

Several writers (Ryle and Strawson, for example) have seen in ordinary language a repository of distinctions sufficient to resolve the difficulties about referring with which this book is concerned. It seems to me certain that careful attention to ordinary language can be illuminating here as elsewhere in philosophy. The complaint of my last chapter is that the authors mentioned have not been careful enough. I try to improve on my predecessors in this respect—to show that Strawson and Ryle and others have overlooked much that could have been of use to them.

# I

# REFERENCE AND
# PHILOSOPHY

1. In 'On Denoting' (1905) there is a well-known passage in which Russell introduces a group of 'puzzles' to which he claims his new theory provides solutions. 'A logical theory may be tested by its capacity for dealing with puzzles, and it is a wholesome plan, in thinking about logic, to stock the mind with as many puzzles as possible, since these serve much the same purpose as is served by experiments in physical science. I shall therefore state three puzzles which a theory as to denoting ought to be able to solve; and I shall show later that my theory solves them.'[1] One of the 'puzzles' which he presents, and it is the one which concerned him most, is formulated in this way. 'Consider the proposition "*A* differs from *B*". If this is true, there is a difference between *A* and *B*, which fact may be expressed in the form "the difference between *A* and *B* subsists". But if it is false that *A* differs from *B*, then there is no difference between *A* and *B*, which fact may be expressed in the form "the difference between *A* and *B* does not subsist". But how can a non-entity be the subject of a proposition? . . . it would appear, it must always be self-contradictory to deny the being of anything. . . . Thus if *A* and *B* do not differ, to suppose either that there is, or that there is not, such an object as "the difference between *A* and *B*" seems equally impossible.'[2]

The problem is somewhat obscured by the formulation. The key passage is this, 'But how can a non-entity be the subject of a proposition? . . . it would appear, it must always be self-contradictory to deny the being of anything. . . .' The difficulty, apparently, is in seeing how, if a thing does not exist, it is possible

[1] *Op. cit.*, p. 47.
[2] *Op. cit.*, p. 48.

to say anything about *it*? For in this case there *is* nothing for our proposition to be about. On the other hand, if there *is* something for the proposition to be about (the proposition is about something), how can it be true to say that the thing does not exist? Of all the problems connected with reference, this is the one that bothered Russell most. He considered it to be the principal achievement of his theory of denoting that it solved this problem. It is not difficult to see why the problem is philosophically interesting. Consider the proposition 'Pegasus does not exist'. It is, we think, both true and about Pegasus. But, on the one hand, it seems that if the proposition is true it cannot be about Pegasus, for what the proposition says is that there is no such thing as Pegasus. On the other hand, it seems that if the proposition is about Pegasus it cannot be true, for then there *is* something for it to be about, viz. Pegasus. So the proposition must be false, for it says that Pegasus does not exist. In face of these difficulties we seem required to admit that contrary to what we had all believed, Pegasus must have being of some kind enabling us to succeed in denying that Pegasus exists.

This is one source of the philosophical interest in this puzzle. It seems to require us to distinguish various ways or varieties of being, and to admit that chimeras, centaurs, and even round squares have being in some sense. In the *Principles of Mathematics* (1903) Russell was convinced by the argument and confidently embraced the consequences.

> *Being* is that which belongs to every conceivable term, to every possible object of thought—in short to everything that can possibly occur in any proposition, true or false, and to all such propositions themselves. Being belongs to whatever can be counted. If $A$ be any term that can be counted as one, it is plain that $A$ is something, and therefore that $A$ is. '$A$ is not' must always be either false or meaningless. For if $A$ were nothing, it could not be said not to be; '$A$ is not' implies that there is a term $A$ whose being is denied, and hence that $A$ is. Thus, unless '$A$ is not' be an empty sound, it must be false—whatever $A$ may be, it certainly is. Numbers, the Homeric gods, relations, chimeras and four-dimensional spaces all have being, for if they were not entities of a kind, we could make no propositions about them. Thus, being is a general attribute of everything, and to mention anything is to show that it is.[1]

[1] *The Principles of Mathematics*, W. W. Norton & Co., New York, 1903, second edition 1937, p. 449.

Russell goes on to explain that existence is not to be confused with being, though he has practically nothing to say as to what the difference is. Zeus has being, but he does not exist. Our argument seems to lead us to a philosophical discovery of the greatest importance. Whole realms of objects denied reality by vulgar common sense are proven to have being of a kind unsuspected by the philosophically naïve. In his lectures of 1910–11, published in *Some Main Problems of Philosophy*, G. E. Moore presents a similar view with all of the *éclat* of an explorer announcing the discovery of a new continent.

> I have already pointed out that to say that a centaur is not real, seems to be equivalent to saying that there is no such thing as a centaur. We should insist most strongly that there really is no such thing; that it is pure fiction. But there is another fact, which seems at first sight to be equally clear. I certainly can imagine a centaur; we can all imagine one. And to imagine a centaur is certainly not the same thing as imagining *nothing*. On the contrary to imagine a centaur is plainly quite a different thing from imagining a griffin, whereas, it might seem if both were nothing—pure non-entities, there would be no difference between imagining the one and the other. A centaur then, it seems, is not nothing: it is something which I do imagine. And if it is *something*, isn't that the same thing as saying that there is such a thing—that it is or has being? I certainly do imagine *something* when I imagine one; and what *is* 'something' it would seem, must *be*—there *is* such a thing as what I imagine. But it would also seem, that 'centaur' is just a name for this something which I do imagine. And it would seem, therefore, that there certainly must *be* such a thing as a centaur, else I could not imagine it. How, therefore, can we maintain our former proposition which seemed so certain, that there is *no* such thing as a centaur?[1]

So reflecting on the problem of how it is possible significantly to deny the existence of Pegasus, or to think about him at all, some philosophers (the early Russell among them) choose one horn of a dilemma which seems to confront them. The dilemma seems to require us to say of 'Pegasus does not exist' either that it is false or that it is not about Pegasus. These philosophers say that, in a sense, it is false. In a sense there is such a thing as Pegasus; he has being. But as is the way with philosophical theories, this solution seems worse than the puzzle it is designed to solve. Five years after the publication of the passage quoted

[1] *Some Main Problems of Philosophy*, Allen and Unwin, 1953, p. 212–13.

above, Russell was in violent revolt against the view it expressed. He was ready to take the other horn of the dilemma—to deny that 'Pegasus does not exist' is about Pegasus.

The former alternative now seemed to him incompatible with his sense of reality. 'The sense of reality is vital in logic,' he says, 'and whoever juggles with it by pretending that Hamlet has another kind of reality is doing a disservice to thought. A robust sense of reality is very necessary in framing a correct analysis of propositions about unicorns, golden mountains, round squares, and other such pseudo-objects'.[1] This passage was written nearly twenty years after the *Principles of Mathematics*. It is, I suppose, understandable that he does not mention his former self as an example of one who had 'juggled' with his sense of reality. In a way which is all too human, instead of criticizing himself, Meinong became the object of this scorn. But that is a story for the next chapter. As to how 'Pegasus does not exist' can fail to be about Pegasus, that was what Russell's Theory of Descriptions was designed to show. But surely if our sense of reality revolts at the thought that Pegasus somehow has being, it revolts equally at the thought that when we say 'Pegasus does not exist' we are not talking about Pegasus. It is not surprising, then, that this problem refused to remain in the grave which Russell dug for it; it has come back from the burial to haunt our philosophical consciences over and over again down the century to our own day.

2. In the case of Russell, the problem of reference derives its philosophical interest mainly from ontology. Frege's interest in the problem, on the other hand, derives from a desire to solve certain problems which arise in connection with the concept of identity. Identity, evidently, is a notion which invites confusion even at the most superficial level, with the ink in the expression '$6 = 3 + 3$'. How, it may be asked, can the statement be true when what is on the right is the sign '$3 + 3$' and what is on the left the sign '6'? The statement says that 6 and $3 + 3$ are identical and, of course, the statement is true, yet 6 and $3 + 3$ are obviously not identical. One need only look to see the difference! Again, 'A student of arithmetic may wonder, e.g., how 6 can be the denominator of $\frac{4}{6}$ and not of $\frac{2}{3}$ when $\frac{4}{6}$ is $\frac{2}{3}$. . . .'[2]

[1] *Introduction to Mathematical Philosophy*, Allen and Unwin, London, 1920, p. 170.
[2] Quine, W. V. *Mathematical Logic*, Harvard University Press, 1951, p. 25.

Frege's concern with identity is not to be located at this superficial level. For all that is involved is a confusion between use and mention, and this was a distinction which Frege was most scrupulous in observing. It is not the signs '$3 + 3$' and '$6$' which are asserted to be identical when we say '$3 + 3 = 6$'. The number 6 is not to be confused with the numerals '6' or 'VI'. '$3 + 3$' and '6' are different designations for the same number, not identical designations as in '$6 = 6$'. Again in '$\frac{4}{6} = \frac{2}{3}$', it is the *ratios* $\frac{4}{6}$ and $\frac{2}{3}$ which are asserted to be identical, not the *fractions* $\frac{4}{6}$ and $\frac{2}{3}$. And ratios unlike fractions do not have denominators.[1]

But even observing the use–mention distinction, identity remains a puzzling notion. Consider the proposition 'Venus is the morning star'. Are we saying that 'Venus' and 'the morning star', different though they be, both refer to the same thing? At one time, Frege tells us, he thought that this view was correct.[2] But he abandoned it because this analysis seemed to turn the proposition 'Venus is the morning star' into a statement about our use of words; for, after all, it is because of the conventions of a community of language users that words refer to the things they do. It is entirely conceivable that in some language other than English the mark (or sounds) 'the morning star' should refer to Mars, and the same is true of 'Venus'. On this analysis then, 'Venus is the morning star' would be true because speakers of English use the expressions 'Venus' and 'the morning star' to refer to the same celestial body. This latter fact is just a consequence of certain conventions which well might have been different. Then it looks as though 'Venus is the morning star' is true because of an 'arbitrary' convention. This conclusion, however, is unacceptable because surely it is the fact that Venus is the morning star which makes our proposition true, and this fact has nothing to do with how we agree to talk. We could not make it otherwise by using *words* differently! Neither can we make it so by talking the way we do!

We are forced to another alternative. When we say 'Venus is the morning star' it is the planet Venus which is said to be identical with the morning star. Nothing is said about the designations 'Venus' and 'the morning star'. But here, too, a difficulty

[1] W. V. Quine, *op. cit.*, p. 25.
[2] Frege, Gottlob. 'On Sense and Reference', in *Translations from the Philosophical Writings of Gottlob Frege*, Philosophical Library, New York, 1952, p. 56.

arises. We are not saying that *two* things are identical, for if we were, our proposition would be false. No *two* things are identical. But if we are not saying that two things are identical it seems that for our proposition to be true, we must be asserting of one thing that it is identical with itself. Then, however, it is difficult to see how our proposition can be informative, for everybody knows that Venus is identical with Venus. On the other hand, it was an astronomical discovery of great importance that Venus is the morning star. The difficulty viewed in this way can perhaps be summarized as follows. Since everything is identical with itself and nothing is identical with anything else, how can an assertion of identity ever be informative? Either what is referred to on one side of the identity sign is the same as what is referred to on the other, in which case one is just saying something uninformative such as '*x* is *x*', or else what is referred to on each side is different, in which case what we are saying is false. But 'Venus is the morning star', and hosts of other assertions of identity are neither false nor uninformative.

Frege concluded, as we shall see, that this puzzle over identity arises through confusion between the sense and the reference of expressions. Russell, as we shall also see, thought that Frege's concept of sense was incoherent and that the difficulty over identity rested on another confusion, that between proper names and definite descriptions. There is still another way out which some have attempted. One might deny that the 'is' of 'Venus is the morning star' is the 'is' of identity. What is then said is that we are not asserting Venus and the morning star to be identical 'in all respects' but only 'equal', or 'identical in some respects'. The difficulty is to make it clear what the distinction between identity and equality is supposed to be in this case, or to explain what 'identity in some respects' is supposed to be if it is not what we ordinarily mean by 'identical in some respects but *not* identical' where this implies that the things in question also differ in some respects. Of course, 'is' does not have this latter sense in 'Venus is the morning star', because there *is* no respect in which Venus and the morning star differ.

3. The notion of identity is central in another of the puzzles which Russell lists among those which any adequate theory of referring ('denoting') ought to be able to solve.

If *a* is identical with *b*, whatever is true of the one is true of the other, and either may be substituted for the other in any proposition without altering the truth or falsehood of that proposition. Now George IV wished to know whether Scott was the author of *Waverley*; and in fact Scott was the author of *Waverley*. Hence we may substitute *Scott* for *the author of 'Waverley'*, and prove that George IV wished to know whether Scott was Scott.

## Digression

Unfortunately Russell's writing on the topics which concern us in this book are plagued with use–mention confusions. The above quotation is a case in point. If *a* is identical with *b*, e.g., Scott is identical with the author of *Waverley*, what we may substitute is certainly not one for the other, for they are the same person! What we substitute in a proposition is 'Scott' (Scott's name) for 'the author of *Waverley*' (the words not the author).

But even this last statement is not free of a confusion like that between use and mention, for how can we substitute a name for a phrase in a *proposition*? A proposition is not a linguistic entity but something 'expressed' by a declarative sentence which is a linguistic entity. It is in a sentence that we substitute a name for the words 'the author of *Waverley*'. What we do is to replace 'the author of *Waverley*' by 'Scott' in a sentence expressing the proposition that George IV wished to know whether Scott was the author of *Waverley*. After making this substitution we get another declarative sentence. This sentence expresses the proposition that George IV wished to know whether Scott was Scott.

Russell's writings on these topics frequently confuse propositions with the sentences which express them. At one point in 'On Denoting', for example, he says, 'The proposition "Scott was the author of *Waverley*" which was written. . . .'[1] But, of course, a proposition is not written. What is written is a sentence expressing that proposition. These distinctions are emphasized here because they are central to the theories both of Russell and Frege. Frege scrupulously observes the distinctions. Russell's writings frequently confuse them. Sometimes this is quite innocuous; the passages can easily be set straight. Sometimes (as we will see) we cannot remedy the confusion without destroying the arguments, since the arguments in these cases rest only upon the confusions!

[1] *Op. cit.*, p. 51.

7

Often what we are concerned with is the proposition expressed by a certain sentence, e.g., the proposition expressed by the sentence, 'Scott is the author of *Waverley*'. We wish to say that propositions, not sentences, are true or false. Thus, given the convention governing the use of quotation marks standardly employed by philosophers, the following form of words is incorrect:

(*a*) 'Scott is the author of *Waverley*' is true.

What we should write instead is

(*b*) The proposition expressed by the sentence 'Scott is the author of *Waverley*' is true.

This is a rather clumsy mode of expression, and once the reader is aware of the distinctions involved, it seems hardly necessary to use it. In what follows I propose to use more natural forms such as (*a*) where there is no danger of confusion. Where there is danger of confusion I will be fully explicit, even at the cost of some awkwardness.

I do not pretend that there are no difficulties over these matters. There are difficulties over the notion of a proposition. A sentence consists of words, but on Russell's view, a proposition also has constituents. What are they? Words cannot be these constituents too, for words are words of some language or other, and propositions are not linguistic entities at all. A proposition may be expressed by an English sentence, but it is not part of English or of any other language. But if words are not the constituents of propositions, what are the constituents? This is a problem which concerned Russell at the time of the creation of the Theory of Descriptions. It also concerned Moore, Meinong, and the young Wittgenstein. Russell changed his mind about it between 1904 and 1910. I do not wish to pursue this question further here, but only to indicate that there is a problem. More will be said about it later. *End of digression.*

4. With the aid of the distinction indicated above we can reformulate our puzzle. 'Scott is the author of *Waverley*' expresses a true proposition. It follows that whatever is true of Scott is true of the author of *Waverley*, yet 'George IV wished to know whether Scott was the author of *Waverley*' expresses a true proposition

8

about the author of *Waverley*, and 'George IV wished to know whether Scott was Scott' expresses a false proposition about Scott.

Thus formulated, the puzzle seems to be about identity rather than about reference. But it can easily be formulated as a puzzle about reference. If we were challenged to justify the substitution of 'Scott' for 'the author of *Waverley*' which gives rise to the difficulty one natural line to take is to say that, after all, the two expressions refer to the same thing according to the first premise of the argument. It follows, then, that the second premise states the same fact as the conclusion, for all that has been changed is that in the second premise Scott is referred to by the expression 'the author of *Waverley*' and in the conclusion by 'Scott'. Surely, it seems an obvious principle governing the notion of reference, that what is true of something is true of it whatever expression we may use to refer to the thing in stating that truth. A rose by any other name would smell the same! Let us call this principle 'the principle of reference'.

All of the philosophers whose views are discussed in this book accept this 'obvious principle'. Quine uses it to conclude that in 'George IV wished to know whether Scott was the author of *Waverley*', the person Scott is not referred to either by 'Scott' or by 'the author of *Waverley*'. These are 'non-designating' occurrences of the expressions. Quine does not question the principle of reference, he denies that the expressions in question refer to anything in the context in question. On the other hand, 'George IV' occurs 'designatively', it does refer to George IV, for any other expression designating him could replace 'George IV' without changing the truth of 'George IV wished to know whether Scott was the author of *Waverley*'. Thus, Quine uses obedience to the principle of reference as the criterion in determining whether a given expression occurs designatively or indesignatively in a given context.

Frege also accepts the principle of reference, but he concludes not that the expressions in question do not designate at all in the premises and conclusion of our argument but that they designate *different* things in each of the premises. The fallacy involved is one of equivocation. Russell accepts the principle, but argues that when properly analysed it is seen that 'the author of *Waverley*' does not occur in the premises at all, so there is nothing for the principle to apply to in the premises in order to arrive at the conclusion.

5. Russell arrives, by way of the law of excluded middle, at the last of the puzzles we will notice. 'By the law of excluded middle, either "*A* is *B*" or "*A* is not *B*" must be true. Hence either "the present King of France is bald" or "the present King of France is not bald" must be true. Yet if we enumerated the things that are bald, and then the things that are not bald, we should not find the present King of France in either list.'[1] Russell, never inclined to solemnity in his work, quips in conclusion, 'Hegelians, who love a synthesis, will probably conclude that he wears a wig.'

The puzzle is that since the present king of France is neither in the list of bald things nor in the list of the things that are not bald, both the proposition stating that he is and the proposition stating that he is not bald are false. But, according to the law of excluded middle, contradictory propositions must have opposite truth-values. Further, these two propositions are contradictory.

This, too, can be viewed as a problem about referring. As in the first puzzle, here we are concerned with a case in which what is referred to does not exist. There the problem was, as to how a proposition referring to what does not exist can be true, if what it states is that the thing referred to does not exist. Here the problem is as to how propositions ascribing characteristics to non-existent things can be false. Russell regards the proposition 'The present king of France is bald' as false, since the present king of France is not on the list of the bald things. 'The present king of France is not bald' is, according to Russell, false as well, and for a similar reason. Russell held all such propositions to be false, but he shows, by his theory, how the law of excluded middle can be saved.

Strawson argues that the statements in question are not false. This is not because, on his view, they are true, but because they are neither true nor false. Of course, this requires him to show that the law of excluded middle is not violated, and he does this according to his own theory. Frege says that such statements as 'the present king of France is bald' occur at all only because of an imperfection in our language. In a scientifically constructed language something would be provided as the reference of 'the

[1] *Op. cit.*, p. 48.

present king of France' and such 'improper' descriptions would be eliminated. Then our propositions would be true or false, depending upon what reference was supplied.

Thus with each of our puzzles we get a host of theories, and these in turn become part of the philosophical subject of referring. There are other problems and other theories not discussed here. What I have done in this chapter is to state the main issues to be presented in this book.

# II

# THE THEORY OF OBJECTS

1. Meinong's theory of objects is rooted in the psychology of Brentano. According to Brentano, a characteristic feature of mental phenomena is 'intentionality' or directedness towards an object. If one sees, one sees something; if one hears, smells, tastes, one hears, smells, or tastes some object. If one opines, supposes, knows, or believes, one opines, supposes, knows, or believes something. Meinong is thus led to see the possibility of a new science or field of knowledge, the theory of objects, for it is evident that there are among existing sciences none 'within which we could attempt a theoretical consideration of the object as such, or from which we could at least demand this'.[1]

But is not metaphysics precisely the discipline we are looking for? Metaphysics takes as its field the study of 'being qua being'. Surely it is in this discipline that we can find a study of objects as such. But, according to Meinong, in spite of the immense reach of metaphysics, it is still not universal enough to encompass the general science of objects. The reason is that metaphysics is confined to what exists. 'However, the totality of what exists, including what has existed and will exist, is infinitely small in comparison with the totality of the objects of knowledge.'[2]

This may easily go unnoticed, says Meinong, because we have a 'prejudice in favour of the actual'. Led by this prejudice, we suppose that what is not real is a 'mere nothing'. We therefore conclude that the non-real is something for which science has no application 'or at least no application of any worth'. That this view is mistaken can be shown by a consideration of 'ideal objects'. Ideal objects do indeed subsist (*bestehen*), but they do not

[1] 'The Theory of Objects', in *Realism and the Background of Phenomenology* (ed.), by R. Chisholm, Free Press, 1960, p. 78.
[2] *Ibid.*, p. 79, all quotations from Meinong are taken from this source.

exist (*existieren*). Consequently, they are not, in any sense, real (*wirklich*). The relations of similarity and difference are examples of ideal objects. They may subsist between realities but they are not 'part of reality' themselves. Our ideas, judgments, and assumptions are often concerned with such objects. Numbers are examples of ideal objects, they do not exist in addition to what is numbered (if what is numbered exists). Sometimes, of course, what is numbered does not exist, for example, we can count the mythological gods on Olympus.

In the new science of objects one important distinction which will be observed and investigated is the distinction between objects 'in the strict sense' and objectives (*objective*). Though all mental acts are directed towards objects, the objects of cognitive acts (knowing, believing, supposing) are of a special kind called 'objectives'.

What we see is an object in 'the strict sense', for example, a cat. But we 'judge' or 'assume' not a cat but, for example, *that the cat is on the mat*, or as Meinong sometimes puts it, we 'judge' *the being of the cat on the mat*. There is, then, besides objects in the strict sense, a special class of objects like *the being of the cat on the mat* or *the non-being of the cat on the mat* which are objects of cognitive acts. If what is judged is true, then the objective of the judgment subsists. The cat and the mat exist, but the objective *the being of the cat on the mat* (*that the cat is on the mat*) does not exist, it subsists.

In a certain sense the objective itself 'can assume the function of an object in the strict sense'. If I judge 'It is true that the antipodes exist' the objective *that the antipodes exist* is related to the objective of my judgment in the same way that the cat and the mat are related to the objective of my judgment 'the cat is on the mat'. 'Truth is ascribed not to the antipodes, but to the objective "that the antipodes exist".' This objective can subsist, but unlike the antipodes themselves, it cannot exist. This is true of all objectives, 'so that every cognitive act which has an objective as its object represents thereby a case of knowing something which does not exist'.

An important contention of Meinong's is formulated in what he calls 'the principle of the independence of so-being (*Sosein*) from being (*Sein*)'. An object's having such and such characteristics is independent of its existence. The round square is round and square, though it does not exist. We may make true or false assertions about what does not exist, e.g., Zeus or Pegasus or the golden mountain. It would be false to say that Pegasus is a duck and true to say he is a horse. But if this is so, the so-being (*Sosein*) of Pegasus must be independent of his being (*Sein*). Pegasus has the characteristic of being a horse independently of whether he exists.

> Any particular thing that isn't real (*Nichtseiendes*) must at least be capable of serving as the object for those judgments which grasp its *Nichtsein*. . . . In order to know that there is no round square, I must make a judgment about the round square. . . . Those who like paradoxical modes of expression could very well say: 'There are objects of which it is true to say that there are no such objects.' (Es gibt Gegenstande, von denen gilt, dass es dergleichen Gegenstande nicht gibt).

Meinong's doctrine of the '*Aussersein* of the pure object' is one of his most difficult, but it is also from the point of view of this book, one of his most interesting and important notions.

> If I say, 'Blue does not exist', I am thinking just of blue, and not at all of a presentation and the capacities it may have. It is as if the blue must have being in the first place, before we can raise the question of its being (*Sein*) or non-being (*Nichtsein*). . . . Blue or any other object whatsoever, is somehow given prior to our determination of its being or non-being, in a way that does not carry any prejudice to its non-being. . . . If I should be able to judge that a certain object is not, then I appear to have had to grasp the object in some way beforehand, in order to say anything about its non-being, or more precisely, in order to affirm or to deny the ascription of non-being to the object.

We have here the idea which is at the root of one of the principal problems about reference presented in our first chapter. Whatever we can talk about must in some sense *be* something, for the alternative is to talk about nothing. Meinong's theory of 'the *Aussersein* of the pure object' is in fact an attempt to provide a solution to that problem about reference. The solution, in effect, is that chimeras, round squares, etc., etc., are objects though nonreal objects; objects 'beyond being and non-being'. This way of putting things is recognized by Meinong himself as 'pretentious'. It can easily be misunderstood. Russell, for example, thought that

Meinong was committed to the view that Pegasus both exists and does not exist. But nothing could be a greater misunderstanding of Meinong's position. He is very careful to make it clear that he is not asserting the existence of round squares and chimeras.

The doctrine that the 'pure object' is 'indifferent to being' (*ausserseiend*) is best viewed as simply recognizing in a rather 'pretentious' way such things as that the subject term of a subject-predicate proposition may very well denote something that does not exist, e.g., Santa Claus. That some propositions about Santa Claus are true and some false is obvious. For example, 'Santa Claus lives at the South Pole' is false. Still, it is a proposition about Santa Claus. Meinong's doctrine of *aussersein* seems to me best interpreted as a recognition of such facts as these: That Santa Claus is denoted by the subject term of the above proposition, that Santa Claus is not Paul Bunyan though neither Santa Claus, nor Paul Bunyan exists. The doctrine of the independence of *Sein* from *Sosein* recognizes the fact that some propositions about Santa Claus and Paul Bunyan are true and some false, though neither Santa Claus nor Paul Bunyan exists.

One of the problems about reference presented in the first chapter becomes, in Meinong's hands, an argument to show that the pure object is *ausserseiend*, beyond being and non-being. The argument is as follows. That $A$ is not (the *Nichtsein* of $A$) is an objective, as much an objective as the being of $A$ (the *Sein* of $A$). The degree of certainty which we are justified in having in asserting that $A$ 'is not' is equal to the degree of certainty which we are justified in having that the objective 'Nichtsein of $A$' has *Sein* (that it has subsistence). An objective can be an objective of being (*Seinsobjektiv*) or an objective of non-being (*Nichtseinsobjektiv*). 'Pegasus exists' asserts an objective of the first kind and 'Pegasus does not exist' an objective of the second kind. Each of these objectives stands in a certain relation to its object, Pegasus. A natural view (a mistaken one according to Meinong) is that the relation of the objective to its object is that of whole to part. The difficulty is that if the whole has being, so must its parts. If we follow the analogy, then we could conclude from the being of the objective, *that Pegasus does not exist* (the non-being of Pegasus), that Pegasus has being. Now there is nothing wrong with this conclusion so long as we do not confuse being with existence. So long as what is asserted is merely that Pegasus has being in some sense or other, though not existence, there is nothing wrong. What Meinong, at one time, was inclined to say was that this argument showed that the object had some third order of being, neither subsistence like the objective nor existence like Plato. This third order of being would belong to every object 'as such'.

Now this third order of being would be different from either subsistence or existence in a special way. Existence is opposed to non-existence. Santa Claus does not, in fact, exist, but he could not subsist. Only ideal objects, numbers, objectives, can subsist. Just as existence is opposed to non-existence, so subsistence is opposed to non-subsistence. The objective *that Santa Claus does not exist*, subsists, but the objective *that Santa Claus exists*, does not subsist. The peculiarity of this third order of being is that it is opposed to nothing. No object can fail to have it. For suppose that there was some variety of non-being opposed to this kind of being, as there is something of the same type as existence and subsistence opposed to them. Then for us to judge that an object had this kind of non-being we would have to ascribe a fourth kind of being to the object, by the same argument used above. We would then be led into an infinite hierarchy of kinds of being. This regress can be stopped by supposing that the object (as such) has a kind of being opposed to nothing. 'The term "Quasisein" seemed to me,' says Meinong, 'for a while to be a completely suitable expression for this rather oddly constituted type of being.' Meinong was himself clearly dissatisfied with this notion of a third kind of being 'in principle unopposed by non-being', whether it was called '*Quasisein*', '*Pseudoexistenz*', or '*Quasitranszendenz*' (all alternatives which he used at one time or another). In his essay 'The Theory of Objects' he thought it best to say that objects 'as such' are '*ausserseiend*', 'beyond being and non-being'. Some of the things which Meinong says here are obscure, but it is certain that Russell's view of Meinong as a man who had embraced chimeras and golden mountains, spirits and round squares, as things which exist in another shadow world is far from true.

2. I see in Meinong's theory of objects (or I think I see) an ontologizing of the logic of our ordinary use of referring expressions. It is clear that Meinong is concerned with the problem as to how it is possible for an assertion which denies the existence

of something to be both true and significant. In denying that the relation of an objective to its object is the relation of whole to part, Meinong rejects one important source of the logical delusion which leads to the problem of negative existentials. There is a problem about negative existential assertions because (and, I believe, only because) we are victimized by a tendency to assimilate referring to some kind of physical act. We cannot hang a man who does not exist, how, then, can we refer to such a man? This can be a problem only for one who (absurdly) fails to see the differences between referring and hanging. The crucial difference, for our purposes, is one which Meinong, as a follower of Brentano, was in an especially good position to see.

There is a famous passage in Brentano's *Psychologie vom empirischen Standpunkt*, in which Brentano attempts to explain his notion of intentionality. J. N. Findlay says of the passage that it '. . . almost attained the position of a *Credo*, inasmuch as all the philosophers who made Brentano's remarkable work the starting-point of their investigations begin their treatises by repeating it or something very like it'.[1] The characteristic which, in Brentano's words, distinguishes psychical phenomena from all others is a property

> . . . which the Schoolmen of the Middle ages called the intentional (or mental) inexistence of an object, and which we although such expressions are not free from ambiguity, should describe as the relation to a content, or the direction to an object (by which we need not understand a reality), or an immanent objectivity. Every mental state possesses in itself something which serves as object, although not all possess their objects in the same way.[2]

This characterization is far from clear, but it is certain that Brentano and his followers understood 'intentionality' in such a way that intentional acts, i.e., mental acts, unlike physical acts, can have non-existent objects. I can think of Santa Claus, though I cannot shake his hand. It is characteristic of mental acts that they are 'directed' to objects, but these objects need not exist. Meinong, as a follower of Brentano, certainly accepted this. He refined and deepened Brentano's analysis. In his theory of objects Meinong

[1] *Meinong's Theory of Objects and Values*, by J. N. Findlay, Oxford University Press, 1963, p. 3.
[2] Quoted in Findlay, *op. cit.*, pp. 3-4.

distinguished between existence and subsistence, and he protested against our 'prejudice in favor of the actual'. It is certain that he rejected what above I called the 'delusion' which leads to the problem of negative existentials. Referring, unlike hanging, can have a non-existent object. But this is not the same as referring to nothing. I would like to think that it was these insights (as well as others) that Meinong was trying to express with his difficult doctrine of the *Aussersein* of the pure object.

I interpret this doctrine of the *Aussersein* of the pure object (the doctrine that the pure object is 'beyond being and non-being') as Meinong's way of expressing his rejection of the argument which leads to the problem of negative existentials. If the pure object (the object 'as such') is beyond being and non-being, then one can deny its existence (or subsistence) whether or not in reality the object exists or has being in any sense. Or put positively, one can refer to anything, whether it exists (or has being in any sense) or not. What one cannot do in talking about objects is to *fail* to refer to something or other. So there is in this doctrine (or I think I can see in it) the recognition of an important distinction which some philosophers such as P. F. Strawson fail to make, viz., the distinction between referring to a non-existent object and failing to refer at all.

Here, then, is one way in which Meinong's views can be seen as an ontologizing of the logic of our ordinary use of referring expressions. Consider again, the principle of the independence of *Sosein* from *Sein*. This asserts that non-existent objects can be truly asserted to have certain characteristics, e.g., Santa Claus has a white beard; the round square is both round and square. That a thing is thus and so (has '*Sosein*') does not entail that it exists (has 'being'). This seems to me to be both correct and plain common sense, though it is incompatible with well-established philosophical theories. It is true that Mr. Pickwick founded a society and false that he operated a meat store. Of course, we may be misunderstood when we say these things. If I tell my child that Santa Claus lives at the North Pole he may be mislead into thinking that Santa Claus really exists. If there is a real chance of this happening I can prevent it by saying, 'Of course, Santa Claus is just make-believe.'

If our assertion that Mr. Pickwick founded a society is not to be misunderstood it must be taken to mean something like, 'In the novel Mr. Pickwick founds a society.' Again in the case of Santa Claus, our assertion must be taken to mean something like, 'According to the myth, Santa Claus lives at the North Pole.' Put in these ways we cancel the implication that Pickwick and Santa Claus are not creatures of fiction and myth. We cancel the implications which mislead children and the ignorant.

It seems to me that in speaking of objects we imply (in some sense) that we are talking about the real world, as opposed to legend, fiction, myth, make-believe, fantasy, etc. Suppose one comes into a room and hears a speaker say, 'My mother bit my leg.' We would be amazed and shocked to hear someone say this just because we would assume that the speaker was talking about the real world and not about his dream. In telling our children about Santa Claus we prefix the account with the words 'according to the myth', just in order to cancel this unwanted implication. So the principle of the independence of *Sosein* from *Sein*, though it captures a part of the logic of our talk about objects also neglects a part. The part which the principle neglects is the implication that in talking about objects we are talking about the real world. It is the ignoring of this implication which makes us feel uneasy in face of the flat statement that an object can have characteristics even though it does not exist.

In talking about objects our audience will take it that we are talking about the real world unless we either warn them that we are not (e.g., by prefacing our remarks with 'according to the legend') or something in the speech context makes it clear that we are not talking about the real world. This explains why an assertion such as 'Santa Claus lives at the North Pole', though true, can mislead. One group of philosophers (the 'inflationists') sees one half of this story; they say correctly that the assertion is true, but to say no more than this is not to tell the whole story. This account does not explain why it is so easy to mislead by telling the truth. Another group of philosophers (the 'deflationists') sees this part of the story and denies that the assertion is either about Santa Claus or true. The doctrine of the independence of *Sosein* from *Sein* can be viewed as a defence of our ordinary ways of talking against the extremists of the deflationist camp.

It seems to me, further, that behind the distinctions of existence and subsistence, ideal objects and real objects which are involved in Meinong's ontology one can detect a recognition of other features of the logic of our ordinary use of referring expressions. I would not, in my own ontology, divide objects into ideal objects which subsist and real ones which exist, but into objects which are, e.g., characters in fiction, legendary figures, mythological figures, comic strip characters, make-believe figures, as well as abstractions, mathematical objects, concepts, etc. If one understands the doctrine of the kinds of being in this way one can even see sense in the view expressed by Russell in 1903 that everything (chimeras, centaurs included) has being of some kind, for chimeras and centaurs, for example, are mythological beings. When we deny the existence of these things we deny the existence of things which have being in these senses. To deny the existence of Zeus is to deny the existence of a mythological being. Even to deny the existence of a round square is to deny the existence of a self-contradictory object. Still one goes too far in saying that everything has some kind of being or other, for how can we place, e.g., the present king of France? To deny his existence is not to deny the existence of a character in fiction, or a mythological creature, or etc., etc.

But if I am right in seeing this much good sense in the theories of Meinong, how wrong the current, standard interpretation of the work of Meinong must be! This interpretation is well expressed in the following estimate of Meinong's work by Gilbert Ryle.

> Meinong was the sort of reformer who makes revolutions inevitable, yet himself stops short of seeing that they are even possible. ... Both in epistemology and in logic, with terrifying assiduity and remarkable rigorousness of reasoning, he carried to their extreme conclusions the implications of presuppositions which no one had yet questioned, and which he himself did not question. But of these conclusions he never said what has to be said, 'By God, this is impossible'. He was perhaps the supreme entity-multiplier in the history of philosophy, and yet, I suppose, the main service which he really rendered philosophy was to force logicians to see that 'wherever possible logical constructions are to be substituted for inferred entities'. ...[1]

Aside from the final remark which so charmingly reflects the time and place of these observations, I think that the view ex-

[1] Gilbert Ryle, *Oxford Magazine*, 26, October 1933, quoted in Findlay, *op. cit.*, p. xiv.

pressed is still the prevalent one. Meinong is the 'supreme entity-multiplier in the history of philosophy'. I hope at least to have shown that another interpretation which brings Meinong's view much closer to common sense than to metaphysical extravagance is possible.

# III

# SENSE AND REFERENCE

1. Frege introduces his distinction between the sense and the reference of names in order to enable him to deal with a puzzle about identity. He opens his 'On Sense and Reference' with this question about it. 'Is it a relation? A relation between objects, or between names or signs of objects?'[1] If we take the first of these alternatives and regard identity as a relation between objects, Frege reasons, then the statement '$a = b$' should mean the same thing as '$a = a$', if '$a = b$' is true. For if '$a = b$' is true, then '$a$' and '$b$' are just two names for the *same* object, and '$a = b$' can tell us no more than '$a = a$'. Identity is a relation in which a thing can stand only to itself and not to another thing. Thus, this interpretation of identity statements must be false because statements of the form '$a = b$' are sometimes highly informative and '$a = a$' never is informative. For example, it was an astronomical discovery of some importance that the morning star and the evening star are one and the same planet.

Nor is Frege able to accept the other of the two alternatives, that identity is a relation between names or signs of objects. Then '$a = b$' would just say that the name '$a$' and the name '$b$' are names for the same thing. This analysis cannot be correct, Frege argues, because the fact that '$a$' is a name for $a$ and that '$b$' is also a name for $a$ results from a purely arbitrary agreement concerning the use of these marks (or sounds). Furthermore, when I say that Venus is the morning star I am conveying information about the heavens, not about our arbitrary use of signs.

Frege now proceeds to his distinction between the sense (*Sinn*)

---

[1] 'On Sense and Reference', in *Translations from the Philosophical Writings of Gottlob Frege*, ed. by Max Black and P. T. Geach, Philosophical Library, New York, 1952. All quotations from Frege are from this source unless specific indication to the contrary is given.

and the reference (*Bedeutung*) of signs. The reference of an expression is the object named or denoted by it. We must distinguish this object from the sense of the expression. The sense of an expression is 'grasped by everybody who is sufficiently familiar with the language'. The sense of a sign, Frege says, contains the 'mode of presentation' whereby the sign gives us its reference. Perhaps the following example will help to clarify the distinction. 'Let *a*, *b*, *c* be the lines connecting the vertices of a triangle with the mid-points of the opposite sides. The point of intersection of *a* and *b* is then the same as the point of intersection of *b* and *c*. So we have different designations for the same point, and these names ("point of intersection of *a* and *b*", "point of intersection of *b* and *c*") likewise indicate the mode of presentation; and hence the statement contains actual knowledge.' So here we can say that the two expressions, 'the point of intersection between *a* and *b*' and 'the point of intersection between *b* and *c*' have the same reference but differ in sense. Similarly, 'the morning star' and 'Venus' have the same reference but differ in sense. Because of this difference, the statement 'Venus is the morning star' conveys 'actual knowledge', and 'Venus is Venus' does not.

'If words are used in their ordinary way,' says Frege, 'what one intends to speak of is their reference. It can also happen, however, that one wishes to talk about the words themselves or their sense.' An example of this occurs when one reports the words of another in *oratio recta* construction. Thus if I say, 'He said "the cat is on the mat",' my words have as their reference the words of the person whose speech is reported, and for this reason, words standing between quotation marks in *oratio recta* construction must not be taken as having their *ordinary* (customary) sense and reference.

In other special constructions Frege held the reference of our words to be their customary sense rather than their customary reference. For example, in the statement, 'Smith knows that Venus is the morning star', the two names 'Venus' and 'the morning star' have their *indirect* reference rather than their *customary* reference. Frege's reason for maintaining this is the following. If in the statement 'Smith knows that Venus is the morning star' the expression 'the morning star' has its *customary* reference (Venus) we ought to be able to replace that expression by any other expression referring to Venus without altering the truth-value of the original statement (*salva veritate*, in the words of Leibniz). But if we replace the expression 'the morning star' by 'the evening star' our statement may change its truth-value, for it is possible that Smith knows that Venus is the morning star and yet does not know that Venus is the evening star. If, on the other hand, we replace the expression 'the morning star' in our statement with another expression having the same customary sense as this expression our statement could not possibly change its truth-value.

Frege concluded that it was this customary sense which was the reference (the *indirect* reference) of the words 'the morning star' in our statement. In general, 'we distinguish accordingly the *customary* from the *indirect* reference of a word; and its *customary* sense from its *indirect* sense. The indirect reference of a word is accordingly its customary sense.'

It should be noted that Frege's argument here rests upon the principle that if two expressions have the same reference, then the one expression may replace the other in any statement in which it occurs, *salva veritate*. Frege explicitly embraces this principle and quotes Liebniz's famous definition in support of it. '*Eadem sunt, quae sibi mutuo substitui possunt, salva veritate.*' The distinction between the *customary* and *indirect* sense and reference of expressions would seem to be imposed on Frege by his adherence to Leibniz's law, for without some such distinction as Frege makes, the 'law' admits counter-examples. For example, expressions occupying positions within clauses governed by such words as 'knows', 'believes', 'thinks', 'supposes' (the so-called verbs of propositional attitude) cannot be replaced in those positions by other expressions standing for the same customary reference, *salva veritate*. The morning star–evening star example above is a case in point. But Leibniz's law is saved once it is pointed out that an expression occupying these positions does not stand for its customary reference, but for its customary sense (its indirect reference).

So far, we have discussed the distinction between sense and reference as it applies to proper names and definite descriptions. But Frege maintains the distinction holds also for the whole declarative sentence containing these names and descriptions. A declarative sentence (spoken in the making of a statement; not, e.g., in fiction or on the stage) has both sense and reference. The customary reference of such a declarative sentence is its truth-value, 'the True' or 'the False'. The sense of the sentence is the thought which it expresses. Frege is most anxious to cancel the psychological connotations of the word 'thought' from his concept of sense, and it is clear that by the 'thought' expressed by a declarative sentence he means what other philosophers call a 'proposition'.

Once again, in view of Frege's adherence to the principle of substitutivity stated above (Leibniz's Law), it will be seen that it is necessary for Frege to extend the distinction between the customary and the indirect sense and reference also to the case of whole declarative sentences. For taking the reference of such a sentence to be always a truth-value, it can be shown that the principle of substitutivity admits of counter-examples. Consider the sentence 'Copernicus believed that the planetary orbits are circles'. Here the words following the word 'that' are a full declarative sentence whose customary reference is 'the False'. But one cannot replace this false statement by *any* false statement *salva veritate*. From the premise that Copernicus believed that the planetary orbits are circular it does not follow that Copernicus believed every false statement.

This conclusion is avoided when it is realized that the sentence 'The planetary orbits are circles' does not have its customary reference in the larger sentence about Copernicus. Here it has its indirect reference, i.e., according to Frege's rule its customary sense, i.e., the proposition that the planetary orbits are circles. What the principle of substitutivity requires is not that the sentence 'The planetary orbits are circles' be replaceable in the sentence about Copernicus by any other sentence standing for the same truth-value but by any other sentence expressing the same proposition. Hence, once the distinction between the customary and the indirect sense and reference is recognized for whole declarative sentences, these paradoxes of substitutivity cannot arise.

It will be useful to show explicitly how and to what extent the theory just described provides solutions for the problems presented in Chapter I. First, let us consider the puzzle about identity statements which led Frege to make his distinction between the sense and reference of names. How can '$a = b$' be both true and different in 'cognitive content' from '$a = a$'? The problem is solved once we see that signs can agree in reference but differ in sense. 'Venus is the morning star' is true, because the two names 'Venus' and 'the morning star' have the same reference, viz., the planet Venus. Yet 'Venus is the morning star' does not express the same proposition as 'Venus is Venus' because 'Venus' and 'the morning star' differ in sense. Since the sense of a declarative sentence (the proposition expressed by it) is a function of the senses of the various signs occurring in that sentence, it follows that the proposition expressed by 'Venus is the morning star' is a different proposition from that expressed by 'Venus is Venus'.

Just as the sense of a declarative sentence is a function of the senses of the various signs occurring in that sentence, so is the reference of such a sentence a function of the references of the signs occurring in the sentence. Since the reference of a declarative sentence is its truth-value, it follows that, for Frege, the truth-value of a declarative sentence will remain unchanged if, in that sentence, we replace a sign by another sign having the same reference. But we must not forget that the reference and (presumably) the sense of a sign changes with the sentential context in which it occurs. Neglect of this consideration leads to puzzles of the kind concerning George IV and the author of *Waverley*. One concludes that since 'Scott is the author of *Waverley*' is true that 'Scott' and 'the author of *Waverley*' are two signs always having the same reference. This is a mistake. They do not have the same reference in 'George IV wished to know whether Scott was the author of *Waverley*'. Their references here are the same as their senses in 'Scott is the author of *Waverley*'. Thus we cannot conclude that George IV wished to know whether Scott was Scott. We may substitute for 'the author of *Waverley*' any other sign having the same reference as it has *in the sentence* 'George IV wished to know whether Scott was the author of *Waverley*' without changing the reference (truth-value) of this sentence. But it is a mistake to substitute 'Scott' for 'the author of *Waverley*' here.

There are features of this solution which may well leave one uneasy. We are told that we may substitute any sign for 'the author of *Waverley*' which has the same reference that it has in the sentence 'George IV wished to know . . .', but we are given no examples of legitimate substitutions of this kind, and one may well wonder how one is to know whether two names have the same reference in an oblique context. This problem reduces, of course, to the problem of specifying an identity condition for

senses. When do two names have the same customary sense? Lack
of clear identity conditions is an infirmity common to so-called
'intensional' objects (propositions, attributes, senses). It is also a
chief ground for the view that we lack really clear conceptions as
to what these purported objects are. The extensionalist's view is
neatly formulated in Quine's dictum 'no entity without identity'.

Frege's view has the disconcerting consequence that a pronoun
within the scope of a verb of propositional attitude (or within the
scope of a logical modality) cannot pick up the reference of an
outlying antecedent outside that scope. Consider, 'Scott was the
author of *Waverley*, although George IV did not know that he was
the author of *Waverley*.' Any name standing in place of 'he' in this
sentence has its oblique reference, though the antecedent of this
pronoun ('Scott') has its ordinary reference in the sentence. How,
then, can the pronoun function? How can it manage to pick up
the reference of its antecedent? Since pronouns function as
bound variables, the difficulty can also be described as a difficulty
concerning the operation of bound variables whose antecedent
quantifiers lie outside the scopes of these peccant verbs. From
'Scott was the author of *Waverley*, although George IV did not
know that Scott was the author of *Waverley*' we cannot infer as we
should expect '($\exists x$) ($x$ was the author of *Waverley*, although
George IV did not know that $x$ was the author of *Waverley*)'. The
inference by existential generalization misfires here because of
Frege's requirement that the name being supplanted by '$x$' in a
sentence containing a verb such as the one we are dealing with
have different references within and without the scope of these
irregular verbs. But then the whole *rationale* of existential generalization is lost for these cases. It would be as absurd to apply
existential generalization here as it would be to infer from 'Winston
Churchill was a popular American novelist of the twentieth
century' and 'Winston Churchill was England's greatest statesman of the twentieth century' that '($\exists x$) ($x$ was a popular American
novelist and England's greatest statesman of the twentieth century)'. The inference is absurd because the subject of these
assertions is not the same person; they merely have the same
name. It is difficult to believe that the inference from 'Scott was
the author of *Waverley*, although George IV did not know that
Scott was the author of *Waverley*' to '($\exists x$) ($x$ was the author of
*Waverley*, although George IV did not know that $x$ was the

author of *Waverley*)', is as absurd as the one involving the name 'Winston Churchill'. Our quantified assertion says no more than 'Someone was the author of *Waverley*, although George IV did not know who that person was', and this seems straightforwardly true in view of the historical facts. It is surprising that Frege, who invented both the semantics of sense and reference and quantification theory, seems to have been unaware of the fact that there is a problem about how the two ideas are to work together.

A further problem concerns the senses of expressions which, in a given context, have their oblique reference. Expressions in such contexts have an oblique sense. But what is that? No examples are given, and if we assume that the ordinary sense of a phrase such as 'the author of *Waverley*' is something like its 'meaning', what are we to think of as its oblique sense? Another meaning? It seems clear, at any rate, that this theory needs working out, but unfortunately Frege has said very little about these topics beyond what is said in this one paper. We will return to these issues later.

It remains to say something about the two remaining problems. How is it possible significantly to deny the existence of Pegasus? Once we see that 'Pegasus' has a sense, we can see that 'Pegasus does not exist' can have a sense (express a proposition), even though 'Pegasus' does not have a reference. Frege thought that sentences of fiction, myth, etc., did express 'thoughts' (propositions). They could do this even though they contained names such as 'Odysseus' which do not have a reference. Of course, such sentences would not have a reference (truth-value), because since the reference of a sentence is a function of the references of the constituent names contained in it, sentences containing names without references would be without a reference themselves.

Once again, one may well feel dissatisfied. It is all right to say that the sentences of a novel do not have truth-values, but there are problems here. One wants to say that 'The home of Ulysses was in Italy' is just false, his home was in Greece. When Homer says that the home of Ulysses is in Greece, what he says is neither true nor false. But when *we* say that it was in Italy what we say is false.

What about Pegasus? Surely 'Pegasus does not exist' is true. But how can it be true for Frege, since he holds that a complex name is without reference if one of its constituent names lacks reference? In a well-constructed language, says Frege, names lacking reference are not to be allowed. In such a language our problem cannot arise, and neither can the problem about the king of France and the law of the excluded middle. That problem arises because the king of France is neither on the list of the bald people nor on the list of the non-bald people. In a 'well-constructed' language 'the king of France' would necessarily occur on one or the other list.

Frege held that existence is a second-level concept, i.e., a concept under which concepts, and concepts only, can sensibly be said to fall. He also held that the sense of what is ordinarily considered a proper name is the same as that of some definite description. Thus, the sense of 'Homer' is perhaps the same as the sense of 'the author of *The Iliad* and *The Odyssey*'. The sense of what is ordinarily considered a proper name varies from person to person, but we can hold the sense of 'Homer' constant for the purposes of our discussion. 'Homer does not exist', correctly understood, must be taken as denying that a certain first-level concept *Author of The Iliad and The Odyssey*, falls under the second-level concept, *Concept under which at least and at most one thing falls*. In other words, 'Homer does not exist' asserts what is asserted by 'It is not the case that one and only one person authored *The Iliad* and *The Odyssey*'. Though this may be true, it does not contain any referenceless names, so the problem of negative existentials cannot arise. I have found no evidence that Frege ever took this problem, which loomed so large for Russell, seriously at all. The solution which I have just offered is never explicitly formulated by Frege as an answer to the problem of negative existentials, rather this solution is a by-product of Frege's treatment of existence as a second-level concept.

It is clear that the problems which were the main concern of Frege were different than those which were of greatest interest to Russell. Frege's central interests in semantics revolved around problems about identity.

2. Our treatment of Frege's doctrines has been largely expository. What follows is, first, a development of Frege's principles. I present and prove six theorems which are entailed by Frege's basic semantical principles. This is followed by a discussion of these consequences, the aim of which is to evaluate Frege's doctrines as a possible semantical theory of a natural language. It

is necessary first to introduce some special terminology. Frege's semantics deals with signs, their senses, and their references. Signs are said to 'denote' (or 'refer to') their references and to 'express' their senses. These technical terms are used to refer to the relation of signs to their senses and their references. There is, however, no term in Frege's writings to stand for the relation of sense to reference. Frege says that the sense is a 'mode of presentation' of the reference. Alonzo Church proposes to say that the sense is a 'concept of' the reference. He adds the warning that '. . . this use of the word "concept" has no analogue in the writings of Frege and must be carefully distinguished from Frege's use of *Begriff*'.[1] In what follows, I adopt Church's terminology. I use the letters '$t$' and '$t'$' to stand for unspecified names, i.e., expressions to which Frege applies the distinction between sense and reference. The expression '. . . $t$ . . .' stands for a complex name containing one or more occurrences of $t$. The expression . . . $t'$ . . . is the same expression as . . . $t$ . . . except that in the former $t'$ has replaced $t$ in one or more of its occurrences in the latter.

In the proofs that follow I appeal to Frege's principle that the reference of a complex name is a function of the references of the constituent names which it contains. Similarly, Frege says that the sense of a complex name is a function of the senses of the constituent names which it contains. Now these functions must be understood as operating in such a way that the sense and reference of these constituent names *alone* does not determine the sense and reference of the complex name in which they occur. The *order* of the appearances of these constituent names is also relevant. An example will illustrate this point. Consider the sentences 'Plato was the teacher of Socrates' and 'Socrates was the teacher of Plato'. The first sentence names the False and the second names the True. It follows (assuming that no proposition can be a concept of more than one truth-value) that these sentences express different senses (propositions). Since the constituent names of both sentences are identical, and the senses and references of these names are identical, it follows that the difference in sense and reference of the whole sentences must be due

---

[1] 'The Need for Abstract Entities in Semantics', by Alonzo Church, reprinted in *The Structure of Language*, ed. by J. Katz and J. Fodor, Prentice Hall Inc., Englewood Cliffs, N.J., 1964. The present quotation is from p. 439 in Katz and Fodor.

to the difference in the order in which these constituent names enter into the two sentences. We must therefore understand Frege's principles in such a way that the relevant functions involve not only sense and reference but also order. Thus . . . $t$ . . . and . . . $t'$ . . . have the same sense and reference whenever $t$ and $t'$ have the same sense and reference, for these contexts are identical except that one contains $t'$ in one or more places where the other contains $t$. One further note on terminology. In what follows I sometimes use the expressions 'c-sense' and 'c-reference' as abbreviations for Frege's terms 'customary sense' and 'customary reference'. Sometimes I use the term 'ordinary' as a synonym for 'customary'.

*Theorem 1.* If $t$ and $t'$ are identical in c-sense they are also identical in c-reference.

*Proof.* Suppose the antecedent of the theorem true and the consequent false. Then since $t$ and $t'$ are not identical in c-reference $t = t'$ is false. But since the antecedent is true, $t = t'$ is identical in sense with $t = t$. This is so because the sense of an expression is a function of the senses of its constituent names, and each sense expressed in $t = t'$ corresponds to a sense expressed in $t = t$ and conversely. But the sense of $t = t$ is a proposition which is a concept of the True. Hence the sense of $t = t'$ is also a concept of the True. Now, assuming that no proposition can be a concept of more than one truth-value, our assumption of the falsity of the theorem leads us to a contradiction, viz., that $t = t'$ expresses a proposition which is both true and false. Hence the theorem is proven.

*Theorem 2.* Expressions identical in c-sense are everywhere interchangeable *salva veritate*.

*Proof.* Let $t$ and $t'$ be identical in c-sense. Suppose that they are not everywhere interchangeable *salva veritate*, i.e., suppose that there exists at least one context . . . $t$ . . . in which $t$ cannot be replaced by $t'$ *salva veritate*. Two cases need to be considered.

*Case 1.* . . . $t$ . . . is an ordinary context. Then under the condition supposed, . . . $t$ . . . and . . . $t'$ . . . differ in truth-value. But this is impossible, since $t$ and $t'$ must be identical in their ordinary references, by Theorem 1. It follows that the references of all of the names in . . . $t$ . . . are identical with the references of all of the names in . . . $t'$ . . . . Then by Frege's principle that the reference of a complex name is a function of the references of its

constituent names, it follows that the references of . . . *t* . . . and
. . . *t'* . . . must be identical, contradicting the assumption.

*Case 2.* . . . *t* . . . is an oblique context. Then under the condition
supposed . . . *t* . . . and . . . *t'* . . . differ in truth-value. But this is
impossible, since the oblique references of *t* and *t'* are their c-
senses. But since by assumption *t* and *t'* are identical in c-sense,
it follows that they are identical in their oblique references.
Hence by the same argument used under case 1, . . . *t* . . . and
. . . *t'* . . . have the same reference thus contradicting the assumption that they differ in truth-value.

This argument depends upon an assumption concerning
Frege's semantics for which I am unable to supply any textual
evidence. Since nothing is said in Frege's writings concerning
this matter, one can legitimately claim that the proof of Theorem
2 is not in accordance with Frege's stated principles.

The questionable assumption upon which the proof of Theorem
2 rests concerns the sense and reference of names which occur in
oblique contexts which are themselves parts of still wider oblique
contexts, i.e., in contexts which are multiply oblique. Such contexts can be thought of as being built up by means of iterated
applications of oblique statement operators to statements. For
example, one such oblique statement operator is 'Smith knows
that'. Application of this operator to the statement 'Venus is the
morning star' produces the singly oblique context, 'Smith knows
that Venus is the morning star'. We may say that the names
'Venus' and 'the morning star' here have degree of obliqueness
one. We can now apply a second oblique statement operator
'Jones believes that', to this last statement in order to produce the
doubly oblique context 'Jones believes that Smith knows that
Venus is the morning star'. We may say that the names 'Venus'
and 'the morning star' here have degree of obliqueness two.
Clearly this nesting of oblique contexts within oblique contexts
can proceed to any degree of complexity. Now there is nothing in
Frege's writing to guarantee that if two names have the same
oblique references in a context of a given degree of obliqueness
they will also have identical references in oblique contexts of any
other degree. Again, there is nothing in Frege's writings
to guarantee that if two names agree in their c-senses, they
must agree in their oblique senses for any degree of obliqueness.

We can now show how these assumptions are involved in the proof of Theorem 2. In case 2 of the proof, oblique contexts are considered generally without concern as to degree. But let us now bring in considerations of degree, and take first an oblique context of first degree. It can be shown by attending to Frege's examples that if two names are identical in c-sense they are also identical in their first-degree oblique references. It follows from this that two names identical in c-sense are everywhere interchangeable in first-degree oblique contexts. Let $t$ and $t'$ be as above, two such terms. Suppose that the first-degree oblique *senses* of $t$ and $t'$ diverge in spite of the fact that their first-degree oblique references are identical. I assume that according to Frege the $n$th-degree oblique reference of a name is its $(n-1)$th-degree oblique sense. This is not simply a generalization of the principle that the oblique reference of a name is its customary sense. The principle is generalized and also extended so as to include consideration of degrees of obliqueness. Suppose, then, that though $t$ and $t'$ agree in c-sense, they disagree in their first-degree oblique senses. Then since the second-degree oblique references of $t$ and $t'$ are their first-degree oblique senses, it follows that $t$ and $t'$ differ in their second-degree oblique references. It follows from this that replacement of $t$ by $t'$ in an oblique context of degree greater than one *may* not take place *salva veritate*, contrary to Theorem 2. This discussion may be summarized as follows. The proof of Theorem 2, under its second case, depends upon the assumption that if two names agree in c-sense they will agree in their $n$th-degree oblique senses for $n \geqslant 1$. We can assume from Frege's examples that if names agree in c-sense they will agree in their first-degree oblique references. But without the first assumption there is no reason to believe that if names agree in c-sense they will agree in oblique reference when they occur in contexts with degree of obliqueness greater than one. The proof of Theorem 2 requires this assumption. On the basis of the second assumption (names identical in c-sense are identical in their first-degree oblique references), we can prove the following restricted case of Theorem 2.

*Theorem 3.* If $t$ and $t'$ are identical in c-sense they are everywhere interchangeable in ordinary and first-degree oblique contexts, *salva veritate*.

*Proof.* Exactly as given for Theorem 2, except that all references to oblique contexts are changed to refer to contexts of first degree of obliqueness.

In view of the above considerations, a question which arises quite naturally is this: Are there any two names which are identical in customary sense? A necessary condition for two names to be identical in c-sense is (according to Theorem 3) that they be everywhere interchangeable in first-degree oblique contexts. Now consider such a context.

(1) Jones denied explicitly that $t = t'$.

Assume that $t$ and $t'$ are identical in c-sense. According to Theorem 3, it follows from (1) that

(2) Jones denied explicitly that $t = t$.

Now going by the ordinary meaning of the expression 'denied explicitly' and the standard accounts of logical possibility, it seems to be a logical truth that (where '$\Diamond$' means 'it is logically possible that')

(3) $\Diamond$ (Jones denied explicitly that $t = t'$ and it is not the case that Jones denied explicitly that $t = t$).

But since on Frege's principles (2) is a logical consequence of (1), it follows that for Frege

(4) $\sim\Diamond$ (Jones denied explicitly that $t = t'$ and it is not the case that Jones denied explicitly that $t = t$).

Since (4) contradicts a logical truth (3), we reject the assumption which leads to (4), viz., that $t$ and $t'$ are identical in c-sense. Since $t$ and $t'$ are any names that can significantly be placed on either side of the identity sign, it follows that no such pair of names can be identical in c-sense.[1] Let us call such names 'singular referring expressions'. We can take the following as proven by the above argument.

*Theorem 4.* No two singular referring expressions are identical in c-sense.

[1] The argument and example were suggested by similar ones in Jonathan Cohen's *The Diversity of Meaning*, Methuen and Co. Ltd., London, 1962, p. 176. It might be contended that (1) and (2) are disguised *oratio recta* constructions involving quoted sentences and that thus the argument fails. I believe any attempt to provide synonymous translations of *oratio obliqua* constructions such as (1) and (2) into *oratio recta* can be shown to be inadequate in view of the arguments presented by Church in 'Carnap's Analysis of Statements of Assertion and Belief', *Analysis*, X, pp. 97-9.

The proof of this theorem requires (1) and (2) to be oblique contexts of degree one. This is plausible, because degree of obliqueness was explained in terms of statement operators ('necessarily', 'Jones believes that', etc.). The intuitive idea behind the notion of degree of obliqueness is that one oblique statement can be nested within another. Now 'Jones denied that' is clearly the kind of statement operator we here have in mind, and there seems to be no way of getting 'explicitly' separated from 'explicitly denied', so that it may function as an operator on statements on its own. Nevertheless, it is the case that Frege says nothing about degree of obliqueness. What we have indicated is that there is a certain gap in his account, and we have tried to fill that gap in a way which seems to be in harmony with other things that Frege says, but there are undoubtedly other ways of developing Frege's principles which would not involve the consequences we have drawn above.

*Theorem 5.* Names which differ in c-reference differ also in c-sense.

*Proof.* By *modus tollens* from Theorem 1.

*Theorem 6.* No sense is a concept of more than one object.

*Assumption.* For any sense and any object of which it is a concept we can form a unique name which expresses that sense (as its c-sense) and whose c-reference is that object.[1]

*Proof.* Suppose that $S$ is a concept of $n$ ($n > 1$) objects, $O_1, O_2, \ldots O_n$. Then by assumption we can form unique names $N_1, N_2, \ldots N_n$ whose c-references are $O_1, O_2, \ldots O_n$ respectively and whose c-sense is $S$. But this contradicts Theorem 5. Hence $S$ cannot be a concept of $n$ ($n > 1$) objects.

*Alternative proof.* This proof is carried through without appeal to Theorem 5.

Every sentence formed by putting any two of $N_1$, $N_2$, $N_n$, in the blanks of '$\ldots = \ldots$' names the False, for no two of these names have the same customary reference. But every sentence so formed is identical in sense with (expresses the same proposition as) $N_1 = N_1$, since each of $N_1, N_2, \ldots N_n$ is identical in c-sense

[1] Theorem 6 could have been taken as an axiom of Frege's semantics and not in need of proof. Thus the strong assumption to which this footnote is appended need not be made. Frege states the principle in *Sense and Reference*, p. 58. Benson Mates takes our Theorem 6 to be a first principle of Frege's semantics, see his *Elementary Logic*, Oxford University Press, 1965, p. 70. See also the article by Church cited in the second footnote to the present chapter, pp. 439–40.

with $N_1$. But $N_1 = N_1$ names the True. Now since no proposition can be the concept of more than one truth-value, it follows that each of the sentences formed by putting any two of $N_1$, $N_2$, ... $N_n$ in the blanks of '... = ...' names the True. But this contradicts what we have just proven. Hence the assumption that $S$ is a concept of more than one object is disproven.

3. In what follows I shall indicate some ways in which these conclusions are significant for an evaluation of Frege's theory viewed as a theory of the semantics of natural languages. According to Theorem 2, names identical in c-sense are everywhere interchangeable *salva veritate*. We have seen this can be proven only on the assumption that names identical in c-sense also are identical in their $n$th-degree oblique senses for any $n$. If c-sense corresponds to meaning, as surely it must if Frege's theory is to be an account of the semantics of natural languages, identity of c-sense corresponds to synonymity. The effect of Theorem 2, thus understood, is to require that synonymous expressions be everywhere interchangeable *salva veritate*. Now this result is surely unacceptable. Some modern philosophers have adopted accounts of synonymity which require synonymous expressions to be everywhere interchangeable *salva veritate* and have then concluded that there are no synonyms in natural languages. Since it is certain that there are synonyms in English, German, etc., it would seem more reasonable to reject an account of synonymity which requires synonyms to be everywhere interchangeable. But Frege's semantics faces this very difficulty in the light of Theorem 2. This would seem to provide motivation for a decision allowing higher-degree oblique senses of expressions identical in c-sense to diverge. Theorem 2 then becomes unprovable. Any Frege-type semantics would still face difficulties over synonymity in view of Theorem 4, for this yields the consequence that no two singular referring expressions are synonymous.

Theorems 4 and 6 together make it impossible, it would seem, for a Frege-type theory to account for one important and pervasive feature of natural languages, i.e., the use of demonstrative expressions and what philosophers have called egocentric words or indicator expressions. Consider the sentence 'That door is closed'. It can be used on different occasions to say of different doors that they are closed. This means that, depending upon the context in which these words are uttered, they can be used to refer to different objects. In Frege's terminology this is to say that the same words 'this door' sometimes refer to one object and sometimes to another. But these words have the same sense (meaning) regardless of the object to which they refer. Now the object to which a name refers is the object of which the sense which it expresses is a concept. It follows by Theorem 6 that 'this door' must always refer to the same object, so long as the context is ordinary. But this is just to say that there can be no such things as demonstrative expressions on Frege's theory. Demonstrative expressions are just those which differ in reference from context to context while retaining a constant meaning. Examples of such words are 'today', 'I', 'you', 'this', 'that', 'here', 'now', etc. What is referred to by these words is communicated by means of non-linguistic clues in the speech context in which they are used, and it is essential to the working of such words that they change their references without changing their meanings. It is a serious defect in a theory of meaning if it makes such a function of words impossible. Unless the argument given above is defective, Frege's theory suffers from this defect.

The difficulty can be brought out in another way by consideration of Theorem 4. According to this theorem, no two singular referring expressions can be identical in c-sense. Now consider the sentences 'This table is brown' and 'That table is brown'. They can be used to say the same thing about the same table (they can, of course, also be used to say the same thing about different tables). But according to Theorem 4 'This table' and 'That table' have different c-senses. Then since the sense of a complex name is a function of the senses of its constituent names, it follows that 'This table is brown' has a different sense from 'That table is brown'. This means that the propositions expressed by these sentences are different. It is difficult to see how Frege can account for the semantics of demonstrative expressions in view of these results. But it can be shown further that these results are contrary to Frege's intentions.

At one point in his essay 'The Thought'[1] Frege turns his

---

[1] 'The Thought', by Gottlob Frege, *Beitrage zur Philosophie des Deutschen Idealismus*, 1918–19. Translated by A. M. and Marcelle Quinton in *Mind*, Vol. LXV, No. 259, July 1956, pp. 289–311. Further references to this paper are to the English translation.

attention specifically to the question with which we have been dealing. The conclusions at which he arrives are incompatible with those which we have shown to be entailed by his theory. This is shown by the following quotation:

> If someone wants to say the same today as he expressed yesterday using the word 'today', he must replace this word with 'yesterday'. *Although the thought is the same* its verbal expression must be different so that the sense, which would otherwise be affected by the differing times of utterance, is readjusted. The case is the same with words like 'here' and 'there'. In all such cases the mere wording, as it is given in writing is not the complete expression of the thought, but the knowledge of certain accompanying conditions of utterance, which are used as means of expressing the thought, are needed for its correct apprehension. The pointing of fingers, hand movements, glances may belong here too. The same utterance containing the word 'I' will express different thoughts in the mouths of different men, of which some may be true, others false.[1]

Now, if what we have shown above is correct the word 'I' cannot refer to more than one person, unless in so doing it changes its sense. This is clearly a possibility not contemplated by Frege. Further, a sentence containing the word 'yesterday' cannot express the same proposition as that same sentence containing the word 'today'. This follows from Theorem 4, together with Frege's principle that the sense of a complex name is a function of the senses of its constituent names.

[1] 'The Thought', *op. cit.*, p. 296. Italics are mine.

# APPENDIX

In this appendix we prove a number of theorems concerning Frege's semantics. They are not directly relevant to the issues dealt with in the body of the chapter. They seem to me to be worth presenting both because of their intrinsic interest and because they illustrate a method of investigation which promises to be fruitful in this area.

The following special symbols and terminology are adopted. They are in addition to those already introduced in the body of the chapter. '$Sn(t)$', '$Sn + 1(t)$', etc., stand for the $n$th, the $(n + 1)$th, etc., degree oblique senses of a name $t$. '$rn(t)$', '$rn + 1(t)$', etc., stand for the $n$th, the $(n + 1)$th, etc., degree oblique references of $t$. Ordinary contexts will be said to have degree of obliqueness zero. Thus '$So(t)$' and '$ro(t)$' stand for the ordinary sense and reference of the name $t$. (As in the body of the chapter, '$t$' and '$t'$' stand for unspecified names.) The principle that the reference of a complex name is a function of the references of its constituent names is called the 'principle of invariance for references'. The analogous principle for senses is called the 'principle of invariance for senses'. The principle that $Sn(t) = rn + 1(t)$ for any $n$, we call the 'principle of inheritance for references'. We adopt the following definitions:

*Definitions.* A complex name . . . $t$ . . . is an *oblique context (name) with respect to an occurrence of one of its constituent names $t$* if, and only if, for some name $t'$, $t = t'$ is true and the result of replacing $t$ by $t'$ at the occurrence in question is that the reference of . . . $t$ . . . changes.

A complex name is *oblique* if, and only if, it is oblique with respect to at least one occurrence of at least one of its constituent names.

The relation of a sense to that object of which it is a sense is the relation of *being a concept*. This relation can be viewed as the

39

relative product of two relations, the relation of expressing and the relation of denoting. The relation of names to the senses they express is called 'expressing'; the relation of senses to the names that express them is the converse of the relation of expressing. Let $C$ stand for the relation of being a concept of an object, let $D$ stand for denoting, and let $\breve{E}$ stand for the converse of the relation of expressing. Then $C$ is the relative product of $\breve{E}$ into $D$. This is written $\breve{E}/D$. $C$, taken in extension, is a class of couples satisfying the condition expressed in the following equation:

$$C = \breve{E}/D = \hat{x}\hat{z}\{(\exists y)(x\breve{E}y) \ \& \ (yDz)\},$$

where $y$ ranges over names in possible languages, $x$ ranges over senses, and $z$ ranges over objects. $D$ is a class of couples satisfying the condition expressed in the following equation:

$$D = E/C = \hat{y}\hat{z}\{(\exists x)(yEx) \ \& \ (xCz)\}.$$

We can derive the following generalized biconditionals from these equations (see the proof of 34.1 in *Principia Mathematica*):

B1. $(x)(z)\{(xCz) \equiv [(\exists y)(x\breve{E}y) \ \& \ (yDz)]\}$

B2. $(y)(z)\{(yDz) \equiv [(\exists x)(yEx) \ \& \ (xCz)]\}$

Let $m$ and $n$ be variables ranging over integers including zero. We can now prove the following theorem.

*Theorem 7*. Two names identical in sense are also identical in reference.

$$(n)(m)(t)(t')\{(Sm(t) = Sn(t')) \supset (rm(t) = rn(t')\}$$

*Proof*. Suppose the antecedent true, that is suppose $N_1$ and $N_2$ to express the same sense $S$. Let $N_1$ denote $r$. We will show that $N_2$ also denotes $r$, thus proving the theorem. From $B_1$ and universal instantiation with respect to $x$ and $z$ we get

$$(\text{1}) \ (\exists y)\{(S\breve{E}y) \ \& \ (yDr)\} \supset SCr.$$

By assumption we have

$$(\text{2}) \ (S\breve{E}N_1) \ \& \ (N_1Dr).$$

By existential generalization, (2) yields

$$(3) \ (\exists y)\{(S\breve{E}y) \ \& \ (yDr)\}$$

From (3) and (1), and *modus ponens* we get

$$(4) \ SCr$$

By Theorem 6, from (4) it follows that $S$ is a concept of $r$ only. Since we assume that $N_2ES$, we get from (4)

$$(5) \ (N_2ES) \ \& \ (SCr).$$

(5) yields, by existential generalization,

$$(6) \ (\exists x)(N_2Ex) \ \& \ (xCr).$$

From $B_2$ and universal instantiation with respect to $y$ and $z$ we get

$$(7) \ (\exists x)\{(N_2Ex) \ \& \ (xCr)\} \supset N_2Dr.$$

From (6) and (7) and *modus ponens* we get

$$(8) \ N_2Dr. \ \text{Q.E.D.}$$

*Theorem 8.* There is at least one name $t$, such that the c-sense of $t$ is not identical with the c-reference of $t$. $(\exists t)(Sc(t) \neq rc(t))$.

*Proof:* Let $t = t'$. Let . . . $t$ . . . be first-degree oblique.

| | |
|---|---|
| (1) $(t)(Sc(t) = rc(t))$ | negation of Th. 8 |
| (2) $Sc(t) = rc(t)$ | (1), U.I. |
| (3) $Sc(t) = r_1(t)$ | principle of inheritance |
| (4) $r_1(t) = rc(t)$ | (2), (3). |

Since $t = t'$, it follows that

| | |
|---|---|
| (5) $rc(t) = rc(t')$ | |
| (6) $Sc(t') = rc(t')$ | (1), U.I. |
| (7) $Sc(t') = r_1(t')$ | inheritance |
| (8) $r_1(t') = rc(t')$ | (6), (7). |
| (9) $r_1(t') = rc(t)$ | (5), (8). |
| (10) $r_1(t) = r_1(t')$ | (9), (4). |

Since $t'$ is any name identical in c-reference with $t$, it follows from line 10 of the proof that $t$ may be replaced in . . . $t$ . . . by any other name identical in c-reference with it without changing the c-reference of . . . $t$ . . . . But since the latter is an oblique context, this is impossible (see definition). Hence the assumption (1) must be rejected and the theorem is proven.

*Theorem 9.* For every $n$ there is at least one $t$ such that the $n$th degree oblique sense of $t$ is not identical with the $n$th-degree oblique reference of $t$. $(n)(\exists t)(Sn(t) \neq rn(t))$.

*Proof.* By weak mathematical induction on the degree of obliqueness.

*Step 1.* $n = 0$. Since the oth-degree oblique sense and reference of $t$ are $Sc(t)$ and $rc(t)$ respectively, the theorem follows for $n = 0$ by Theorem 8.

*Step 2.* By *reductio ad absurdum* of the conditional, $(\exists t)(Sn(t) \neq rn(t)) \supset (\exists t)(Sn + 1(t) \neq rn + 1(t))$.

| | |
|---|---|
| (1) $(\exists t)(Sn(t) \neq rn(t))$ | hypothesis of induction |
| (2) $(t)(Sn + 1(t) = rn + 1(t))$ | premise |
| (3) $Sn(t) \neq rn(t)$ | (1), E.I. |
| (4) $Sn + 1(t) = rn + 1(t)$ | (2), U.I. |
| (5) $(t)(rn + 1(t) = Sn(t))$ | inheritance |
| (6) $rn + 1(t) = Sn(t)$ | (5), U.I. |
| (7) $Sn + 1(t) = Sn(t)$ | (4), (6). |
| (8) $rn + 1(t) = rn(t)$ | (7), Theorem 7 |
| (9) $Sn(t) \neq rn + 1(t)$ | (3), (8). |
| (10) $(sn(t) \neq rn + 1(t))$ & $(Sn(t) = rn + 1(t))$ | (9), (6). |

Since line 10 is a contradiction, the premise must be rejected and Step 2 of the induction is proven.

*Theorem 10.* There is at least one name $t$, such that the c-sense of $t$ is not identical with the $n$th-degree oblique sense of $t$, for any $n \geqslant 1$. If $n \geqslant 1$, then $(\exists t)(Sc(t) \neq Sn(t))$.

*Proof.*

| | |
|---|---|
| (1) $(t)(Sc(t) = Sn(t))$ | premise |
| (2) $rc(t) = rn(t)$ | (1), U.I., and Theorem 7. |

Let $t = t'$ and let ... $t$ ... be an oblique context which is $n$-degree oblique for any $n \geqslant 1$. It follows that

| | |
|---|---|
| (3) $rc(t) = rc(t')$ | |
| (4) $rc(t') = rn(t')$ | (1), U.I. Theorem 7. |
| (5) $rn(t) = rc(t')$ | (2), (3) |
| (6) $rn(t) = rn(t')$ | (4), (5). |

Line 6 leads to a contradiction, just as does line 10 of the proof of Theorem 8. Therefore we reject the premise and the theorem is proven. If $n = 0$ the theorem asserts a contradiction.

*Theorem 11.* For every $n$ there is at least one $t$, such that the $n$th-degree oblique sense of $t$ is not identical with the $(n + 1)$th-degree oblique sense of $t$. $(n)(\exists t)(Sn(t) \neq Sn + 1(t))$.

*Proof.* By weak mathematical induction on the degree of obliqueness.

*Case 1.* $n = 0$. Since $Sc(t) = So(t)$, the theorem is proven for $n = 0$ by Theorem 10. By Theorem 10, $(\exists t)(Sc(t) \neq S1(t))$.

*Case 2.* By *reductio ad absurdum*, we prove the conditional, $(\exists t)(Sn - 1(t) \neq Sn(t)) \supset (\exists t)(Sn(t) \neq Sn + 1(t))$

| | |
|---|---|
| (1) $(t)(Sn(t) = Sn + 1(t))$ | premise |
| (2) $Sn(t) = Sn + 1(t)$ | (1), U.I. |
| (3) $rn(t) = rn + 1(t)$ | (2), Theorem 7 |
| (4) $Sn - 1(t) = rn(t)$ | inheritance |
| (5) $(\exists t)(Sn - 1(t) \neq Sn(t))$ | hypothesis of induction |
| (6) $Sn - 1(t) \neq Sn(t)$ | (5), E.I. |
| (7) $Sn(t) = rn + 1(t)$ | inheritance |
| (8) $Sn - 1(t) \neq rn + 1(t)$ | (6), (7) |
| (9) $Sn - 1(t) \neq rn(t)$ | (8), (3) |

Since (9) and (4) contradict each other, the premise is rejected, and the conditional is proven.

*Theorem 12.* There is at least one name $t$ such that the c-reference of $t$ is not identical with the $n$th-degree oblique reference of $t$ for any $n \geqslant 1$. If $n \geqslant 1$, $(\exists t)(rc(t) \neq rn(t))$.

*Proof.*

| | |
|---|---|
| (1) $(t)(rc(t) = rn(t))$ | premise |
| (2) $rc(t) = rn(t)$ | (1), U.I. |

Let $t = t'$ and let . . . $t$ . . . be $n$-degree oblique for any $n \geqslant 1$. Then

| | |
|---|---|
| (3) $rc(t) = rc(t')$ | |
| (4) $rc(t') = rn(t')$ | (1), U.I. |
| (5) $rn(t') = rn(t)$ | (2), (3), (4) |

Line 5 leads to a contradiction in the same manner as does line 10 in the proof of Theorem 8. Therefore we reject the premise and the theorem is proven. $n$ carries the same restriction upon it here as it does in Theorem 10, and for the same reason.

Some of the above theorems supply answers to questions raised by other writers on Frege's semantics. In *Meaning and Necessity*, Rudolf Carnap makes the following observations about Frege's distinction between the customary and the oblique senses of names: 'It is not easy to say what his reasons were for regarding them as different. . . . It does not appear, at least not to me, that it would be unnatural or implausible to ascribe its ordinary sense to a name in an oblique context.'[1] And further he says of the oblique sense, 'Incidentally, it seems that Frege nowhere explains in more customary terms what this third entity is'.[2] We have proven in Theorem 10 that customary and oblique senses cannot, on Frege's principles, be identified. We have proven, further, that the first-degree oblique sense of a name must not, in general, be identified with its second-degree oblique sense (see Theorem 11). If there is a problem as to what this 'third entity' (the first-degree oblique sense) is, it is even more difficult to say what this fourth entity (the second-degree oblique sense) is.

But further, it can be shown that the number of entities which Frege's theory requires us to distinguish is denumerably infinite. It is to a discussion of this problem that I now turn. Carnap has maintained that it is a serious disadvantage of Frege's theory of sense and reference that it requires the existence of an infinity of entities of a totally unfamiliar kind. 'Then Frege's method leads, further, to an infinite number of entities of new and unfamiliar kinds; and, if we wish to be able to speak about all of them, the language must contain an infinite number of names for these entities.'[3] Again he says, 'The greatest complexity would result from the use of the Frege–Church method, according to which an expression has infinitely many senses depending upon the text.'[4] In *Meaning and Necessity* Carnap offers the following proof of the above assertions:

> Let us start with a name $n$, say the sentence '$Hs$'. According to Frege's method, there is an entity, $e_1$, named by this name; this is

---

[1] *Meaning and Necessity*, by Rudolf Carnap, University of Chicago Press, 2nd edn., 1955, p. 129.
[2] *Ibid.*, p. 129.
[3] *Ibid.*, p. 130.
[4] *Ibid.*, p. 232.

the truth-value of '$Hs$'. And there is another entity, $e_2$, which is the sense of '$Hs$'; this is the proposition that Scott is human. This proposition $e_2$ may also have a name; if we wish to speak about it, we need a name for it. This name is different from $n$, because the latter is the name of $e_1$ and hence, in a well constructed language, should not be used simultaneously as a name of another entity. Let the new name be $n_2$. Like any name, $n_2$ has a sense. This sense of $n_2$ must be different from the nominatum of $n_2$; it is a new entity, $e_3$, not occurring in customary analyses. In order to speak about $e_3$ we need a new name, $n_3$. The sense of $n_3$ is a new entity $e_4$; and so forth *ad infinitum*.[1]

Now the first thing to observe about this argument is that it is fallacious. Consider the name $n_2$, which has as its reference the sense of the name $n_1$. As Carnap observes, $n_2$ has a sense. He says that this sense is a 'new entity', $e_3$. But Carnap's argument is fallacious just because he offers no proof that $e_3$ is a new entity. He offers no argument to show that $e_3$ is not the same 'entity' as $e_1$. Carnap is certainly right in thinking that Frege's method involves us in the use of an infinite number of descriptive phrases of the kind 'the sense of $n_1$', 'the sense of $n_2$', etc. What is lacking is a proof that the references of these descriptions are none of them identical with each other. It is hardly a criticism of Frege's semantics that it requires an infinite number of descriptive phrases of the kind indicated. It is a basic principle of Frege's semantics that the oblique reference of a name is its ordinary sense. Thus we have two descriptive phrases of the kind in question, 'the ordinary sense of $n$' and 'the oblique reference of $n$', which have the same reference.

Nevertheless, something like Carnap's contention is true. Frege is committed to distinguishing an infinite number of classes of senses of different kinds.[2] I will now prove this contention. Notice that I am not claiming, as Carnap does, to prove that every name must have an infinite number of distinct senses associated with it, but only that it is a consequence of Frege's

[1] *Meaning and Necessity*, by Rudolf Carnap, University of Chicago Press, 2nd edn., 1955, p. 130.

[2] The argument which follows rests upon an assumption about the hierarchy of senses and references. The assumption is that the $n$th-degree oblique sense of no name is identical with the $m$th-degree oblique sense of any *other* name, if $m \neq n$. Since the hierarchy is not to be found in Frege, but is an extension of his ideas, the sentence to which this footnote is appended should be understood as qualified in this sense.

principles that there exists an infinite number of distinct kinds of senses. The crucial lemma which yields this result is stated in the following theorem.

*Theorem 13.* $(n)(m)(l)\{[(n \neq 0)$ & $(l \neq 0)$ & $(n = m + l)] \supset$
$[(\exists t)(Sm(t) \neq Sn(t)]\}$

First, I will explain the significance of the conditions on the numerical subscripts. *n*, *m*, and *l* are variables ranging over the integers including zero. The antecedent of the conditional generalized in Theorem 13 requires that *n* be a positive integer greater than *m* by the amount *l*, where *m* may be zero and where *l* cannot be zero. The theorem states that for any such *m*, *n*, and *l* there exists at least one name *t*, such that the *m*th-degree oblique sense of *t* is not identical with the *n*th-degree oblique sense of *t*. It can easily be seen how Theorem 13 yields the result I am claiming to establish. Suppose $m = 0$ and $l = 1$. Then the theorem yields the result that for some name *t* the customary sense of *t* (i.e., the 0th-degree oblique sense of *t*) is not identical with its first-degree oblique sense. This is to say that the class of customary senses of names is not identical with the class of first-degree oblique senses of names, so there exists at least two non-empty classes of oblique senses of different degrees. The theorem can now be used to establish the non-identity of the class of first-degree oblique senses and the class of second-degree oblique senses. It can also be used to establish the non-identity of the class of customary senses and the class of second-degree oblique senses. We have thus proven the existence of three non-empty classes of oblique senses of different degree. This process can obviously be repeated to establish our conclusion: *There exists a denumerable infinity of non-empty classes of senses of different degrees of obliqueness.*

Now for the proof of Theorem 13. It will be given informally and by considerations best presented in terms of the following diagram:

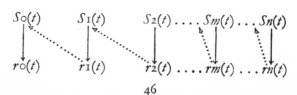

The proof is by *reductio ad absurdum*. Assume the negation of Theorem 13. This is the following:

$$(1) \; (\exists n)(\exists m)(\exists l)\{[n \neq 0 \; \& \; (l \neq 0) \; \& \; (n = m + l)] \; \& $$
$$[(t)(Sm(t) = Sn(t))]\}$$

Now by existential instantiation we can specify the variables $m$, $n$, and $l$ for specific integers (say $m$, $n$, and $l$) and drop the three existential quantifiers in front of the formula (1). We can now simplify the result to obtain

$$(2) \; (t)(Sm(t) = Sn(t)).$$

Now specify the universally quantified variable for some name, say $t$. We get the formula

$$(3) \; Sm(t) = Sn(t).$$

By Theorem 7 it follows that $rm(t) = rn(t)$ (see diagram). From this and the principle of inheritance it follows that $Sm - 1(t) = Sn - 1(t)$. Again, by Theorem 7, the references corresponding to these senses shown by the solid arrows in the diagram are identical. The senses shown corresponding by the broken arrows to these latter references are also therefore identical by the principle of inheritance. It is clear that we will finally arrive at the result

$$(4) \; ro(t) = rl(t)$$

Now we make two assumptions. One is that there is a name $t'$ such that

$$(5) \; t = t'.$$

The second assumption is that we have some context $\ldots t \ldots$ in which $t$ has its $l$th-degree oblique sense, i.e., $\ldots t \ldots$ is an $l$-degree oblique context.

From (2) it follows that

$$(6) \; Sm(t') = Sn(t').$$

The same reasoning which led from (3) to (4) leads from (6) to

$$(7) \; ro(t') = r1(t').$$

From (5) follows

$$(8) \; ro(t) = ro(t').$$

From (4), (8), and (7) follows

$$(9)\ rl(t) = rl(t').$$

From (9) it follows by the principle of invariance for references that $t'$ may replace $t$ in the context $\ldots t \ldots$ without change of reference. But since $t'$ was an arbitrary name which satisfied the condition of being identical in customary sense with $t$, it follows that any such name may replace $t$ in the context $\ldots t \ldots$ without changing the reference of $\ldots t \ldots$. But this contradicts the assumption that $\ldots t \ldots$ is an oblique context (see definition). Thus the theorem is proven by *reductio ad absurdum*.

Theorem 13 yields our result only on assumptions about the hierarchy of sense and reference as described at the beginning of this appendix (see footnote 2 on p. 45). A result much closer to Carnap's can be obtained by making the very natural assumption that the truth-values, the True and the False, are not senses. Starting with any (declarative) sentence, we are led to 'an infinite number of entities of new and unfamiliar kinds'. We can make use of this diagram in establishing this conclusion.

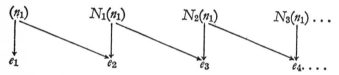

Let $n_1$ be a (declarative) sentence; $N_1(n_1)$ a first-degree oblique context containing $n_1$; $N_2(n_1)$ a second-degree oblique context containing $n_1$, etc., *ad infinitum*. The vertical arrows represent the denoting relation and the diagonal arrows the expressing relation. Since $n_1$ is a sentence, $e_1$ is a truth value. The sense of $n_1$ is a proposition $e_2$. The reference of $n_1$ within the context $N_1(n_1)$ is (by the principle of inheritance) the entity $e_2$ again. The sense of $n_1$ within the context $N_1(n_1)$ is its first-degree oblique sense $e_3$; $e_3$ is the reference of $n_1$ within the context $N_2(n_1)$. Continuing thus, we generate an infinite sequence of entities of 'new and unfamiliar kinds'. The assumption that any two of these entities are identical is incompatible with the assumption that no truth-value is a sense. This can be shown by repeated application of Theorem 7 and the principle of inheritance in the same manner as was involved in the proof of Theorem 13.

# IV

# RUSSELL'S THEORY OF DESCRIPTIONS

1. An 'incomplete symbol' for Russell is an expression which 'does not have any meaning in isolation'. It must be defined 'in certain contexts'. Examples of what Russell calls 'incomplete symbols' are the connectives of the propositional calculus. The defined connectives in *Principia Mathematica* are introduced by what are called 'contextual definitions'; these connectives are given a 'definition in use'. Thus conjunction is defined in terms of the primitive connectives $\sim$ and $V$, by the definition $(p \ \& \ q) = \sim(\sim p V \sim q)Df$ and the material conditional is introduced by means of the contextual definition $(p \supset q) = (\sim p V q)Df$. What is being defined is conjunction (&) and the material conditional $\supset$, but what appears in the definiendum in each of these definitions is not the sign & or $\supset$ by itself, 'in isolation'. What appears are the expressions $p \ \& \ q$ and $p \supset q$ containing the defined signs as parts. They are defined 'contextually'. Russell says that what is given meaning by the definitions are not the signs & and $\supset$, but these signs in the contexts $p \ \& \ q$ and $p \supset q$.

Russell held that certain expressions must be defined contextually because they have no meaning 'by themselves', though they 'contribute to the meaning' of the sentences in which they occur. These signs are given contextual definitions because they are 'incomplete symbols', they are not incomplete symbols because they are given contextual definitions. In the case of definite descriptions Russell offered a proof that they were incomplete symbols. Still it is not at all clear what an incomplete symbol is. His 'proof' that descriptions are incomplete symbols is, in fact, a proof that they are not what he calls 'proper names'. These latter are paradigms of 'symbols' which are not incomplete, though he

49

does not call them 'complete symbols'. I do not know whether Russell thought that every 'symbol' was either a proper name (in his sense) or an incomplete symbol, though his 'proof' that descriptions are incomplete symbols implies that he thought this. Russell's account of proper names is clearer than his account of incomplete symbols. Since they are paradigms of what incomplete symbols are *not*, it will help us to understand the one notion if we examine the other.

2. 'A name,' says Russell, 'is a simple symbol, directly designating an individual which is its meaning, and having this meaning in its own right, independently of the meanings of all other words.'[1] This statement leaves much in need of explanation. What does it mean to say that a symbol 'directly designates' an individual? What does it mean to say of a 'symbol' that it has its meaning 'in its own right' and 'independently of the meanings of all other words'? But though there is a problem as to what it means to say that a 'symbol directly designates an individual', it is clear that for Russell this individual is the meaning of the name. The thing which has the name (the 'bearer' of the name) is the meaning of the name. Russell further assumes that in any subject–predicate proposition the meaning of the subject term is the thing denoted (or referred to) by this term.

Starting from these assumptions, the problem arises as to how we can make assertions which are true (and therefore significant) about what does not exist. If we assert 'Socrates is wise' we may analyse our assertion as saying of a certain individual (the meaning of the name 'Socrates') that he has the characteristic of being wise. It follows from Russell's assumptions that if this individual does not exist the assertion is meaningless because its subject term is meaningless. Thus the object denoted by the subject term of a subject–predicate proposition must exist if the subject term is a proper name. How, then, can we assert significantly, for example, that the round square does not exist? This assertion cannot be analysed as saying that there is a certain object (the meaning of the expression 'the round square') which has the characteristic of not existing; for then the assertion would be a contradiction asserting both that there is a certain object and that

[1] *Introduction to Mathematical Philosophy*, p. 173.

it does not exist. There is nothing which is the meaning of the phrase 'the round square'. It seems to follow, paradoxically, that if the proposition is true it is meaningless. Russell concluded that the grammatical similarity between 'Socrates is wise' and 'The round square does not exist' covers a vast difference in the logical forms of these two propositions. 'The round square does not exist' cannot be analysed as being a subject–predicate proposition, the meaning of whose subject term is the round square.

The conclusion can be generalized. Consider any (significant) proposition such that: (1) it is apparently of the subject–predicate form, and (2) the apparent subject term denotes something which does not exist. This apparent subject term cannot be a proper name, for if it were the proposition would be meaningless. Russell assumes that the only possible subject terms of propositions genuinely of the subject–predicate form are proper names. Thus it follows that propositions satisfying conditions (1) and (2) above are not genuinely of the subject–predicate form. In Russell's words these points are put in this way, 'Whenever the grammatical subject of a proposition can be supposed not to exist without rendering the proposition meaningless, it is plain that the grammatical subject is not a proper name, i.e., not a name directly representing some object. Thus in all such cases, the proposition must be capable of being so analyzed that what was the grammatical subject shall have disappeared.'[1]

Notice that Russell is making two assumptions: (1) that the meaning of a name is the bearer of the name, and (2) that the subject term of a genuine subject–predicate proposition is, in all cases, a proper name. The first assumption is explicitly made; the second is not. The reasoning of the last paragraph clearly requires this second assumption.

3. The assertion 'The round square does not exist' is an example of an assertion which could not be true if what is denoted by the grammatical subject exists. It follows that 'the round square' is not a proper name in our assertion. It follows from this, together with the assumption that the only genuine subject terms are proper names, that 'the round square' will not appear as the grammatical subject of the assertion which gives the analysis, and displays the true logical form, of the one under consideration.

[1] *Principia Mathematica*, Vol. I, 2nd edn., Cambridge University Press, 1925, p. 66.

Russell says that the proper analysis of the proposition 'The round square does not exist' is given by the proposition 'It is not the case that there is one and only one object which is both round and square'. In *Principia* the symbol $(\imath x)(Qx)$ represents a definite description, an expression of the form 'the so-and-so'. The symbol can be read 'the (unique) $x$ which has the property $Q$'. In the case of any proposition of the form 'The (unique) $x$ which has the property $Q$ does not exist', Russell's theory offers as the analysis a proposition of the form

$$\sim\{(\exists c)(x)[(Qx) \equiv (x = c)]\}.$$

The expression within the scope of the negation sign says that one, and only one, thing has the property $Q$. Thus, on Russell's view, the assertion that the so-and-so does not exist is analysed as saying that it is not the case that one, and only one, thing has the property so-and-so. Conversely, the assertion 'The so-and-so exists' is analysed by the proposition 'One, and only one, thing has the property so-and-so'. The proposition 'The so-and-so exists' is symbolized in *Principia* by the expression $E!(\imath x)(Qx)$. One of the two contextual definitions which introduce definite descriptions into *Principia* enables us to eliminate them from propositions of the form $E!(\imath x)(Qx)$.

14.02 $E!(\imath x)(Qx) = (\exists b)(x)[(Qx) \equiv (x = b)]Df.$

There is no doubt something odd about the assertions 'The round square does not exist', 'The Queen of England exists'. Ordinarily we would perhaps say 'There is no such thing as the round square' or 'England is a monarchy and its monarch is a queen'. Russell would maintain, I believe, that these are but stylistic variants of 'The round square does not exist' and 'The Queen of England exists', having the same logical powers as these latter. For present purposes, the important thing to notice about the definition 14.02 is that it enables us to eliminate the definite description from any context of the form $E!(\imath x)(Qx)$. The proposition into which this one is analysed contains no definite description. In Russell's words, the description has 'disappeared on analysis'. Russell's theory of descriptions offers us an analysis which enables us to eliminate descriptive phrases from any context in which they occur.

4. By an argument like the one used to show that 'The round square' does not function as a proper name in the assertion 'The round square does not exist', Russell attempts to prove that $(\imath x)(Qx)$ is an incomplete symbol in every context in which it occurs. Consider the proposition expressed by the sentence 'Scott is the author of *Waverley*'. 'The author of *Waverley*' is of the form $(\imath x)(Qx)$, it is $(\imath x)$ ($x$ wrote *Waverley*). The word 'is' here, according to Russell, is the so-called 'is of identity'. Let us assume that in our sentence 'the author of *Waverley*' is a proper name. Then there is some object, call it '$c$', which is 'directly designated' by this name. Then 'Scott is the author of *Waverley*' means the same as 'Scott is $c$'. Now there are two possibilities: (1) either Scott is not identical with $c$, in which case 'Scott is $c$' is false, or (2) Scott is identical with $c$, in which case 'Scott is $c$' means the same as 'Scott is Scott', and is a tautology. Therefore, if 'the author of *Waverley*' is a proper name, 'Scott is the author of *Waverley*' is either false or tautological. But it is both true and not tautological, therefore 'the author of *Waverley*' is not a proper name in our sentence.

Russell's conclusion is that 'the author of *Waverley*' means nothing. It cannot mean $c$, and it cannot mean anything other than $c$. But since everything is either $c$ or other than $c$, 'the author of *Waverley*' means nothing. What Russell's argument proves is that descriptions are not proper names in his sense. He shows this by showing that the meaning of a definite description cannot be the thing it 'describes'. To conclude from this that descriptive phrases 'mean nothing' is to go beyond what has been shown. It is to assume that the meaning of a descriptive phrase, if it has a meaning, is the thing it 'describes'. But this assumption is not (and cannot be) justified.

Furthermore, a brief consideration of the above argument reveals that it is circular. Russell asks us to consider the proposition expressed by the sentence

(1) Scott is the author of *Waverley*.

But there is no such thing as *the* proposition expressed by these words. On Russell's theory there are at least four different propositions that (1) might be used to express. (1) might be understood as containing (beside the copula) either (*a*) two proper names, or a proper name and a description. This name might be

(b) 'Scott' or (c) 'The author of *Waverley*'. A fourth possibility (d) is that (1) consists of two descriptions, one disguised and the other explicit. It is perfectly clear that (c) and (d) are excluded in the above argument for Russell is clearly assuming that in (1), 'Scott' is functioning as a proper name and not as a disguised description. This still leaves alternatives (a) and (b). Now it cannot be alternative (a) which is the correct one, for if (1) contains two proper names the proposition which it expresses would be trivial and mean the same as 'Scott is Scott', which, according to Russell, it does not. This leaves us with alternative (b). According to this alternative, Russell's proposition is the one expressed by (1) when it is understood to contain a definite description to the right of the copula. But if it is assumed from the beginning that 'the author of *Waverley*' in (1) is a definite description and not a proper name, then we are assuming the very thing which it is the aim of the proof to establish.

Another way to bring out the circularity of Russell's argument is this. At a certain point in that argument he rejects an assumption on the ground that that assumption has the consequence that (1) means the same as 'Scott is Scott'. But how can Russell know that the proposition expressed by (1) is not this trivial one unless he is assuming that in (1) 'the author of *Waverley*' is not functioning as a proper name in his sense? And if he is assuming this, what is the point of proving it?

Another of Russell's arguments is this. The proposition expressed by the sentence 'Scott is the author of *Waverley*' cannot be analysed as saying that 'Scott' and 'the author of *Waverley*' are two names for the same person. For if that were what the proposition asserts, what would be required for it to be true is that someone should have named Scott 'the author of *Waverley*', and if someone had named Scott 'the author of *Waverley*', then Scott would have been the author of *Waverley*, even though he did not, in fact, write *Waverley*. If, on the other hand, no one had named him 'the author of *Waverley*' the assertion 'Scott is the author of *Waverley*' would be false, even though, in fact, Scott had written *Waverley*. On the other hand, since Scott did write *Waverley*, he is the author of *Waverley*, even if no one ever named him 'the author of *Waverley*'. And if someone had named him 'the author of *Waverley*' he would not have been the author of *Waverley*, if he had not, in fact, written *Waverley*. Russell concludes, 'Thus the proposition "Scott is the author of *Waverley*" is not a proposition about names, like "Napoleon is Bonaparte"; and this illustrates the sense in which "the author of *Waverley*" differs from a true proper name.'[1] Since descriptions are not proper names, they have no meaning 'in isolation'. It is for this reason that Russell introduces them into *Principia* by contextual definitions.

This striking and elegant argument is fallacious, though its conclusion is correct. There is no reason, in logic, why Scott should not have been named 'The Author of *Waverley*'. (Perhaps his father hoped that his son would some day write a novel called '*Waverley*'.) If he had been thus named, and if someone (in the appropriate circumstances) had asked, 'Who is that man?', it would have been true to say of Scott, 'He is The Author of *Waverley*.' It would have been true to say this whether or not Scott had actually written *Waverley*. It would have been true, though it might well have been misleading, for the hearer might misunderstand the speaker and suppose that he was saying that Scott had written *Waverley*. Indeed, if I wished to tell you that Scott was the author of *Waverley* I would just say, 'Scott is the author of *Waverley*.'

It is more difficult to be misled in this manner in the written than in the spoken language, for in writing one uses upper-case letters, 'The Author of *Waverley*' rather than 'the author of *Waverley*' to mark the distinction we are indicating. Thus nothing Russell says proves that if one says 'He is the author of *Waverley*' one could not be telling you Scott's name, just as one is if (in the appropriate circumstances) he says 'He is Walter Scott'.

But it is precisely because we can mislead in this way that we do not name our children 'The Author of *Waverley*' or 'The Mayor of London'. If I were introducing a son of mine so-named you might think that I had said that he was the present mayor of London. These difficulties can be avoided either by using, as names for persons, names which are not words of our language at all, such as 'Joseph', 'Mary', 'Jane', or names such as 'Grace' and 'Charity' which, because they stand for abstract things do not, in context, lend themselves easily to the kind of confusions we have been considering. (But compare 'Charity looks desirable' with 'Mary looks desirable'.) There is another relevant characteristic of the examples we have given. They are all common proper names.

[1] *Principia Mathematica*, Vol. I, 2nd edn., Cambridge University Press, 1925, p. 67.

If one wants to give one's child a novel name one had better make it up, like 'Revilo'. If one chooses a word (or group of words) in our language one may be inconvenienced by constantly having to warn one's audience off the wrong interpretation of one's words.

5. We have presented the contextual definition of $E!(\imath x)(Qx)$. Let us now examine the other context in which $(\imath x)(Qx)$ can occur, $U(\imath x)(Qx)$. Propositions of this latter form say of the so-and-so that it has the property such-and-such. The fact that there are these two kinds of propositional contexts into which definite descriptions enter and not just one, reflects the view that existence is not one among the properties which things may or may not possess.

Let us turn then to the analysis of propositions of the form $U(\imath x)(Qx)$. Consider Russell's example, 'The author of *Waverley* was a poet'. According to Russell, this entails three propositions: (1) at least one person authored *Waverley*; (2) at most one person authored *Waverley*; (3) whoever authored *Waverley* was a poet. The conjunction of these three propositions 'define', according to Russell, what is meant by the proposition 'The author of *Waverley* was a poet'. In the *Introduction to Mathematical Philosophy* he tells us that this means that 'The author of *Waverley* was a poet' both logically entails and is entailed by the conjunction of these three propositions; they are logically equivalent. In general, any proposition of the form $U(\imath x)(Qx)$ entails (1) $(\exists x)(Qx)$, and (2) $(x)\{(y)[(Qx) \ \& \ (Qy) \equiv (x = y)]\}$ (1) states that at least one thing has the characteristic $Q$ and (2) states that at most one thing has $Q$. The conjunction of (1) and (2) is logically equivalent to $(\exists c)\{(x)[(Qx) \equiv (x = c)]\}$. And this is the definiens of the definition 14.02 for $E!(\imath x)(Qx)$. Therefore $E!(\imath x)(Qx)$ is entailed by every proposition of the form $U(\imath x)(Qx)$. What is further entailed is that the unique thing which has the characteristic $Q$ also has the characteristic $U$. Thus we get the second of the contextual definitions which introduce definite descriptions into *Principia*:

$$14.01 \ U(\imath x)(Qx) = (\exists b)[(x)((Qx) \equiv (x = b)) \ \& \ (Ub)]Df.$$

6. When a proposition of the form $U(\imath x)(Qx)$ is itself a part of a larger proposition Russell says that the description has a secon-

dary occurrence in the larger proposition. When the description has a secondary occurrence in a proposition that proposition does not entail that the thing 'described' exists. The proposition from which $(\imath x)(Qx)$ is to be eliminated is called the 'scope' of $(\imath x)(Qx)$. If $(\imath x)(Qx)$ is to be eliminated from the entire proposition containing it, then $(\imath x)(Qx)$ is said to have a 'primary' occurrence in that proposition. Some examples will be of help. Consider the proposition:

(1) The king of France is not bald.

This is ambiguous, for it may be taken as being of the form

(2) $\sim\{(\exists c)((x)[(Qx) \equiv (x = c)] \,\&\, U(c))\}$

in which case it does not entail $E!(\imath x)(Qx)$. Or (1) may be taken as being of the form

(3) $(\exists c)[(x)((Qx) \equiv (x = c)) \,\&\, (\sim U(c))]$

in which case it does entail $E!(\imath x)(Qx)$.

It is necessary, therefore, to distinguish those cases in which the entire proposition is of the form $U(\imath x)(Qx)$ from those in which $U(\imath x)(Qx)$ is itself a part of the whole proposition containing the description. In order to indicate the scope of $(\imath x)(Qx)$, Russell adopts the convention of placing $[(\imath x)(Qx)]$ before the part (or the whole) which is taken as being of the form $U(\imath x)(Qx)$. The definition 14.01, which was given above, should contain a scope operator and appears in *Principia* in this way:

14.01 $[(\imath x)(Qx)]U(\imath x)(Qx) = (\exists c)(x)[(Qx) \equiv (x = c) \,\&\, (Uc)]Df.$

The scope operator can be thought of as accompanied by brackets thus

$[(\imath x)(Qx)]\{\ \ \}.$

The definition 14.01 requires us to eliminate the description from the entire proposition enclosed within these brackets. Returning to the above example, if (1) is interpreted as (2) it will be symbolized as

(4) $\sim[(\imath x)(Qx)]U(\imath x)(Qx).$

And if (1) is interpreted as (3) it will be symbolized as

(5) $[(\imath x)(Qx)]\{\sim U(\imath x)(Qx)\}.$

7. When $E!(\imath x)(Qx)$ is true the description $(\imath x)(Qx)$ behaves like a proper name for purposes of logic. It is not in general true that

$$\{(x)(Ux)\} \supset \{U(\imath x)(Qx)\}.$$

For example, it does not follow from

$$(x)(x = x)$$

that

$$(\imath x)(Qx) = (\imath x)(Qx).$$

What is true of everything is not necessarily true of $(\imath x)(Qx)$, for $(\imath x)(Qx)$ may not exist! But if $(\imath x)(Qx)$ exists, then what is true of everything is true of $(\imath x)(Qx)$. This is expressed in a theorem of *Principia*.

14.18 $\{E!(\imath x)(Qx)\} \supset \{[(x)(Ux)] \supset [U(\imath x)(Qx)]\}.$

Russell comments on this theorem, 'That is to say, when $(\imath x)(Qx)$ exists, it has any property which belongs to everything.'

In view of the above account there should be no difficulty in seeing that the following is also a theorem.

14.21 $\{U(\imath x)(Qx)\} \supset \{E!(\imath x)(Qx)\}.$

The symbolism of *Principia* allows us to associate $E!$ with definite descriptions, but that sign cannot appear in the context $E!x$. There are, according to Russell, good philosophical reasons for this. He says, 'When in ordinary language or in philosophy, something is said to "exist", it is always something described, i.e., it is not something immediately presented, like a taste or a patch of colour, but something like "matter" or "mind" or "Homer" (meaning "the author of the Homeric poems"), which is known by description as "the so-and-so", and is thus of the form $(\imath x)(Qx)$. Thus in all such cases the existence of the (grammatical) subject $(\imath x)(Qx)$ can be analytically inferred from any true proposition having this grammatical subject. It would seem that the word "existence" cannot be significantly applied to subjects immediately given; i.e., not only does our definition give no meaning to $E!x$ but there is no reason, in philosophy, to suppose that a meaning of existence could be found which would be applicable to immediately given subjects.'[1]

[1] *Principia Mathematica*, Vol. I, 2nd edn., Cambridge University Press, 1925, pp. 174-5.

Russell says that the authors of *Principia* are justified in giving no sense to $E!x$ or $\sim E!x$ because the assertion 'x exists' or 'x does not exist' is senseless when 'x' is replaced by a proper name. Russell holds that of course it does make sense to say 'Pegasus does not exist', but that is because 'Pegasus' is not a proper name but a disguised description. That 'Pegasus' is not a proper name follows from the fact that Pegasus does not exist. Hence 'Pegasus' cannot mean Pegasus, for then it would be meaningless. What it means to say 'Pegasus does not exist' depends upon what description the speaker 'has in mind' when he says this, perhaps it means 'The winged horse of Greek mythology does not exist'. For Russell, most of what are ordinarily called proper names are really disguised descriptions.

8. It may be the case that what, for one person, is a proper name is, for others, a disguised description. Since the meaning of a name is its bearer, to know the meaning of a name is to know its bearer. To know the bearer of a name is, for Russell, to be acquainted with the bearer. Now since we are not all acquainted with the same things, what is for one person a proper name of $x$ may not be, for another, a name of $x$ at all. What is a name for one person may be a description for another. It may seem that there well might be difficulty in two such people understanding each other. Russell is apparently not disturbed by this. He thinks that so long as what is a name for the one person names the same thing that is described by what is a description for the other there will be no difficulty.

I do not see how, on Russell's theory, these difficulties can be avoided. Suppose that you are 'acquainted' with John F. Kennedy and I am not. When you hear the assertion 'John F. Kennedy is dead' this will certainly mean something different to you than what it means to me. What it means to me depends on what description 'John F. Kennedy' is a 'disguise' for in my case. Maybe it is a 'disguise' for 'the husband of Mrs. Kennedy'. Then 'John F. Kennedy is dead' means to me that the husband of Mrs. Kennedy is dead. It does not mean that to you. Further, suppose that in a third case the description is a disguise for 'the father of John–John'. Then 'John F. Kennedy is dead' in this third case means that the father of John–John is dead. It would thus seem to be only in the case of a lucky accident that two people would mean the same thing by 'John F. Kennedy is dead'. These consequences are absurd, but I do not know how Russell can avoid them.

It is to Russell's credit that he recognizes a difficulty here, but his attempt to deal with it is very unsatisfactory. If we say, e.g., 'Bismarck was an astute diplomatist', according to Russell, we '. . . intend to make our statement, not in the form involving the description, but about the actual thing described . . . we should like, if we could, to make the judgment which Bismarck alone can make, namely, the judgment of which he himself is a constituent'.[1] But we cannot make this judgment because, being unacquainted with Bismarck, we cannot use an expression which means in such a 'judgment', Bismarck. We would not 'know' the meaning of an expression which 'means' Bismarck, and any proposition containing such an expression would be meaningless for us.

What we know, however, is that there is 'an object B' called 'Bismarck', and we know that B was an astute diplomatist. 'We can thus *describe* the proposition we should like to affirm, namely, "B was an astute diplomatist", where B is the object which was Bismarck. What enables us to communicate in spite of the varying descriptions we employ is that we know there is a true proposition concerning the actual Bismarck, and that, however we may vary the description (so long as the description is correct), the proposition described is still the same. This proposition, which is described and is known to be true, is what interests us; but we are not acquainted with the proposition itself, and do not know *it*, though we know it is true.'[2] What I find incoherent in this is the idea of a proposition which we know to be true but which we cannot understand. This proposition is the one we 'intend to make'. How can we intend to make a proposition we cannot understand? How can we possibly know such a proposition to be true?

It seems to me that there is a special difficulty for Russell's views on this topic in connection with non-extensional contexts. What is for me a proper name is not, in general, a proper name for you. Suppose, then, that I say something of the form $f(a)$

---

[1] *Mysticism and Logic*, Longmans, Green & Co., 1925, London, p. 218. Chapter X, 'Knowledge by Acquaintance and Knowledge by Description', republished in this volume, was first published in 1910.
[2] *Ibid.*, p. 218.

where $a$ is a proper name for me. My assertion $f(a)$ must then, on Russell's views, mean something different for me from what it means for you. What it means for you will be expressed by a sentence involving some definite description, say $f(\imath x)(Qx)$. Now two cases need to be considered. (1) $a = (\imath x)(Qx)$ is not true. This case involves a special kind of misunderstanding. You thought that I was referring to $(\imath x)(Qx)$ and I was not. This kind of misunderstanding certainly occurs in connection with our use of proper names and is easily enough corrected. (2) This is the usual case, $a = (\imath x)(Qx)$. That is, you get the reference correct. Further, if $f$ represents an extensional predicate, what I mean when I say $f(a)$ is materially (though not, in general, logically) equivalent with what you understand by $f(\imath x)(Qx)$. Now, though this makes it look as though the *normal* situation in human communication involves misunderstanding, Russell can face this result of his theory with equanimity for the following reason. What you understand has the same truth-value as what I mean, and we are talking about the same thing, for $a = (\imath x)(Qx)$. On Russell's view, then, the normal situation with regard to human communication involves misunderstanding, but not so great a misunderstanding as to keep us from communicating truths about a commonly understood object of reference.

But now let '$f$' stand for a non-extensional predicate. Suppose I hear George IV say, 'I wonder if Scott is the author of *Waverley*.' Suppose that for me and for George IV 'Scott' is a proper name in Russell's sense. Suppose I now say to you, 'George IV wants to know if Scott is the author of *Waverley*.' Suppose, finally, that for you 'Scott' is not a proper name but a disguised description. What you understand by what I said will be expressed with the use of a description which expresses what 'Scott' means for you. Let that description be 'the author of *Ivanhoe*'. Now what you understand is expressed by the sentence 'George IV wants to know if the author of *Ivanhoe* is the author of *Waverley*'.

The situation just represented presents a difficulty for the following reason. Even though, in fact, Scott is the author of *Ivanhoe*, it is perfectly possible that George IV does not know this. Let us suppose that George IV does not know that Scott wrote *Ivanhoe*. Then what you understand is not even materially equivalent with what I meant when I said, 'George IV wants to know if Scott is the author of *Waverley*.' What you understand by these

words is false. It would be the merest accident if what you understand in such a situation were to be materially equivalent with
what I mean. (It just happens to be the case that George IV also
wants to know if Scott is the author of *Ivanhoe*.) No matter what
description 'Scott' disguises for you, the normal situation will be
one in which what I mean by 'George IV wants to know if Scott
is the author of *Waverley*' is true and what you understand by
these words is false. Since the same argument can be repeated for
non-extensional predicates generally, we may conclude that
Russell's theory faces a serious difficulty if viewed as a theory of
communication in natural languages. The difficulty is as to
how it is possible, on Russell's views, for communication to
take place when what is being reported are the beliefs, wants,
hopes, in a word the 'propositional attitudes', of a third
person.

9. Throughout this chapter it has been assumed that there is no
problem as to what is meant by the phrase 'definite description'.
For all that he has to say about definite descriptions, Russell has
very little to say as to what a definite description is. He says that
it is an expression of the form 'the so-and-so'; that it is an expression of the form $(\imath x)(Qx)$, and he says that this last is to be
read 'the (unique) $x$ that has the property $Q$'. At the beginning of
'On Denoting' he explains the notion of a definite description by
giving a list of examples. '. . . the present King of England, the
present King of France, the centre of mass of the solar system at
the first instant of the twentieth century, the revolution of the
earth round the sun, the revolution of the sun round the earth',
these are all what Russell in 1905 called 'denoting phrases'. They
are what he later came to call 'definite descriptions'. After listing
these examples he says, 'Thus a phrase is denoting solely in virtue
of its *form*.'[1]

In each of the three accounts mentioned above the notion of
'form' is crucial. What does it mean to say of a phrase that it is of
the form 'the so-and-so'? The most obvious response to this
question is that the form of a phrase is a matter of grammar.
Strawson, for example, talks about '. . . phrases beginning with
the definite article followed by a noun, qualified or unqualified, in

---

[1] 'On Denoting', reprinted in *Logic and Knowledge*, p. 41.

the singular'.[1] He says that this is the class of expressions with which Russell's Theory of Descriptions is concerned. And he thinks that the phrases so-described are 'expressions of the form "the so-and-so" '.

To show that there is a problem here we can begin by pointing out that there are many phrases which fit Strawson's description (they begin with the definite article and are followed by a singular noun which is 'qualified or unqualified'), which certainly are not definite descriptions, e.g., 'the table', in the proposition 'The table is the most important article of furniture in a dining room'. Here what is wrong is that the phrase 'the table' is not being used to refer to some particular table. Then consider the proposition, 'The book is on the table.' Suppose that this proposition is expressed in a context in which the phrase 'the table' does refer to some particular table. Here there is some inclination to say that 'the table' is a definite description, but if we do say this we abandon the view that a phrase is a descriptive phrase in virtue of its grammatical form, because the phrase 'the table' has the same grammatical form in the proposition in which it is a definite description and the one in which it is not.

I think that 'form' cannot be understood as grammatical form in the account of definite descriptions. Consider the proposition '*The Vicar of Wakefield* is behind the desk'. If the words 'The Vicar of Wakefield' are used to refer to the novel they are the name of the novel, not a description. But if the words are used to refer to the Vicar they are a description, not a name. But only one phrase is involved, not two. Thus the distinction cannot be one of grammatical form.

But clearly not any expression used to refer to a unique object is a definite description, e.g., proper names are not definite descriptions.

It seems to me that whether a phrase is or is not a definite description (in a given proposition) depends on the logical form of that proposition, on how the proposition is to be analysed. If the proposition is correctly analysed in a certain fashion it contains a definite description, otherwise not. Clearly, 'The Eternal City' in 'The Eternal City welcomed the new Pope' is not a descriptive phrase. The proposition does not entail that there exists

---

[1] 'On Referring', reprinted in *Essays in Conceptual Analysis*, ed. by A. G. N. Flew, Macmillan Co., London, 1956, p. 21.

one, and only one, city which is eternal. But if the only way to decide whether a given expression functions as a definite description is to see whether or not Russell's analysis of such propositions is the correct one in the case in question it would follow that Russell's analysis cannot be mistaken and that those, like Strawson, who have argued that it is mistaken are confused over a definition.

10. It remains for us to state how the apparatus and distinctions involved in the theory we have expounded provide solutions to the problems presented in the first chapter. First the puzzle about George IV's curiosity. In 'On Denoting' Russell says, 'The puzzle about George IV's curiosity is now seen to have a very simple solution. The proposition "Scott was the author of *Waverley*" which was written out in its unabbreviated form in the preceding paragraph, does not contain any constituent "the author of *Waverley*" for which we could substitute "Scott".' Russell's view is apparently this. One derives the conclusion from the premises of this argument by substituting a proper name for a description on the basis of a true statement of identity having that proper name and that description flanking 'is'. But on his analysis of propositions containing descriptive phrases, the description being replaced does not actually occur in the premise in which the substitution is made. It is only a kind of logical mirage which causes us to think that 'the author of *Waverley*' is a 'constituent' in the proposition 'George IV wanted to know whether Scott was the author of *Waverley*'. Analysis shows that it is not a constituent, for the phrase 'the author of *Waverley*' disappears on analysis. Therefore this phrase cannot properly be replaced by 'Scott', for the phrase is not really there to be replaced.

There is, in my opinion, much that is obscure in this account, but since the whole of the following chapter is devoted to a discussion of Russell's treatment of this puzzle, I will not discuss it further at this point.

That part of the account which concerns the notion of the 'scope' of a definite description is employed by Russell in providing a solution to the puzzle about the present king of France and the law of the excluded middle. The proposition expressed by the sentence

(1) The present king of France is bald.

is unambiguous and is of the form

$$(2)\ U(\imath x)(Qx).$$

Since this entails $E!(\imath x)(Qx)$, (1) is false. Hence the negation of (1), according to the law of the excluded middle, is true. But, 'The present king of France is not bald' is ambiguous. It is this fact which creates the puzzle. The ambiguity arises from the fact that the descriptive phrase may have either a primary or a secondary occurrence in 'The present king of France is not bald'. If this is interpreted as according a primary occurrence to 'the present king of France' it will be false, since like (1) it also entails that there is one, and only one, present king of France. Hence, on this interpretation, 'The present king of France is not bald' is not the contradictory of (1). The true contradictory of (1) is the proposition 'The present king of France is not bald', when this is interpreted as according a secondary occurrence to the descriptive phrase, for then it denies that one, and only one person, is both at present king of France and bald; and this last is true if (1) is false. Hence the law of excluded middle is preserved.

Next we can see how it is possible to deny the existence of something without falling either into nonsense or self-contradiction. Consider 'Pegasus does not exist'. 'Pegasus' is not a proper name but a disguised description. Suppose the description which it represents is 'The winged horse captured by Bellerophon'. Now when we analyse 'The winged horse captured by Bellerophon does not exist' according to Russell's theory it becomes 'Either nothing is winged and a horse and was captured by Bellerophon or more than one thing was'. Here the descriptive phrase has disappeared. Thus there can be no problem as to how the subject of the proposition 'Pegasus does not exist' can denote a non-existent object. The proposition does not really have a subject. It is really the denial of an existential generalization. The proposition is neither about Pegasus nor about the winged horse captured by Bellerophon, there are no such things. 'Pegasus does not exist' is really a proposition to the effect that either nothing has certain characteristics or more than one thing has, but nothing non-existent is named in it.

Finally, Russell's theory shows us how statements of identity can be both true and non-tautological. They can be so by having at least one definite description flanking the identity sign. If the identity sign is flanked only by proper names the assertion is either tautological or false. But in significant and true assertions of identity there must be a descriptive phrase. The statement of identity then turns out really to be an existential generalization and thus significant.

# V

# EXTENSIONALITY AND DESCRIPTIONS

1. (1) Scott is the author of *Waverley*. (2) George IV wished to know whether Scott was the author of *Waverley*. Therefore (3) George IV wished to know whether Scott was Scott. Why does this conclusion not follow from the premises? Russell introduced this puzzle in 'On Denoting'. He said it was one of '. . . three puzzles which a theory as to denoting ought to be able to solve'. He also said of these three puzzles, '. . . I shall show that my theory solves them'.[1] He accepts the principle of substitutivity which is appealed to in passing to the conclusion from the premises, but Russell holds that the argument is only apparently of the form sanctioned by the principle.

This principle is formulated as follows, 'If *a* is identical with *b*, whatever is true of the one is true of the other, and either may be substituted for the other in any proposition without altering the truth or falsehood of that proposition.'[2] There is use–mention confusion in this formulation. We will return to it later, for it is significant.

When we rewrite the premises (1) and (2) in accordance with Russell's theory the definite description 'disappears on analysis'. Thus there is no definite description to be replaced by 'Scott'. The puzzle is caused by a logical mirage. This is Russell's solution. 'The puzzle about George IV's curiosity is now seen to have a very simple solution. The proposition "Scott was the author of Waverley", which was written out in its unabbreviated form in the preceding paragraph, does not contain any constituent "the

[1] 'On Denoting', reprinted in *Logic and Knowledge*, Allen and Unwin, London, 1956, p. 47.
[2] *Ibid.*, p. 47.

author of *Waverley*" for which we could substitute "Scott".'[1]
There is a mistake here. (3) cannot be obtained by substituting
'Scott' for 'the author of *Waverley*' in (1). We must make this
substitution in (2). I assume that Russell meant to say this and
that it is this substitution to which he objects.

2. The 'solution' is inadequate. The premises contain no definite
description after it has been eliminated in accordance with
Russell's analysis. But how does this show that the propositions
(1), (2), (3) when thus analysed do not constitute a valid argument? After all, sometimes we can substitute proper names for
descriptions in propositions (apparently) containing them. Such
substitutions are sanctioned by a theorem of *Principia*:

$$14.15 \; \{(\imath x)(Qx) = b\} \supset [U(\imath x)(Qx) \equiv U(b)].$$

Russell must have been thinking of principles such as this when,
after offering the above 'solution', he said, 'This does not inter-
fere with the truth of inferences resulting from making what is
verbally the substitution of "Scott" for "the author of *Waverley*",
so long as "the author of *Waverley*" has what I call *primary* occurrence in the proposition considered.'[2] Now consider any argument such that its first premise is of the form of the protasis of
14.15, its second premise of the form of the left- and the conclusion of the form of the right-hand side of the apodosis. Re-
written in accordance with Russell's theory, this argument contains no descriptions, and it is valid. 14.15 itself contains no
descriptions when expanded in accordance with the contextual
definitions which introduce descriptions into *Principia*. What,
then, is wrong with the view that the argument (1), (2), (3) is
sanctioned by 14.15? The answer cannot be that given by the
logical mirage account. It is true that (1), (2), (3) when analysed
contains no descriptions, but the same is true of 14.15.

What is wrong with the view under consideration is that the
descriptive phrase is required to have primary occurrence in both
of the propositions in which it appears in 14.15, but it has primary
occurrence only in the first premise of (1), (2), (3). What Russell
tells us in the above quotation is that in any proposition in which
'the author of *Waverley*' has a primary occurrence, we may validly

[1] 'On Denoting', reprinted in *Logic and Knowledge*, Allen and Unwin, London, 1956,
pp. 51–2.
[2] *Ibid.*, p. 52.

replace it by 'Scott' (assuming (1), of course). But then it appears that Russell has abandoned the logical mirage theory in the very paragraph in which he presents it. Now we are told that what is wrong with replacing 'the author of *Waverley*' by 'Scott' in (2) on the basis of (1) is that the description does not have a primary occurrence in (2).

3. Russell does not tell us why the interpretation of (2) which sees in it a primary occurrence of the description (hereafter I call this 'the primary interpretation') is wrong. But it is wrong, for (2) on this interpretation entails that *Waverley* was not co-authored. If *Waverley* had been co-authored it would not, on the primary interpretation, be logically possible that George IV wished to know whether Scott was the author of *Waverley*. But no plausible analysis of our proposition (hereafter '(2)') can have this as a consequence. A sufficient condition for the truth of (2) is that George IV should have asked, in all seriousness, 'Is Scott the author of *Waverley*?' Now surely he could have seriously asked this question though *Waverley* had been co-authored. What is the proof that this queer consequence does follow on the present interpretation of (2)? On this interpretation (2) is of the form:

$$(4)\ (\exists c)\{(Qx) \equiv_x (x = c)\ \&\ (Uc)\}.$$

(4) is an existentially generalized conjunction, so that we can distribute the existential quantifier to each of its conjuncts. Now simplifying by eliminating the right conjunct we get:

$$(5)\ (\exists c)\{(Qx) \equiv_x (x = c)\}.$$

This by the definition 14.02 of *Principia* is the definitional expansion of:

$$(6)\ E!(\imath x)(Qx).$$

Consistently with the interpretation we have supplied for the variables above, this says,

(7) One, and only one, person wrote *Waverley*.

And (7) entails that *Waverley* was not co-authored.

This result brings out in a particularly revealing way what it is that the primary interpretation misses. It misses the feature of (2) which makes it 'intentional' in the technical sense. 'Intentional' verbs behave in a characteristic way as concerns the existence of their objects. It is not possible to take a bath in a non-existent tub. But it is possible for someone to want to take a bath in my tub, even though I do not, in fact, possess one. Just so, George IV could not have assaulted the author of *Waverley* if *Waverley* had been co-authored, but he could have wanted to know if Scott was the author of *Waverley* though *Waverley* had been co-authored and even if no such book as *Waverley* had ever been written.

Thus the primary interpretation of (2) is not a correct one, and we escape the conclusion that (1), (2), (3) is a valid argument.

We turn then to the alternative interpretation which Russell's theory provides for (2), the secondary interpretation. (2) now is taken to be of the form:

$$(8)\ X[(\imath x)(Qx)]U(\imath x)(Qx).$$

The sign '$[(\imath x)(Qx)]$' in (8) is the 'scope operator', and in this formula it indicates that the descriptive phrase is to be eliminated from the subordinate proposition '$U(\imath x)(Qx)$' and not from the whole of (8). That is, the result of eliminating the description from (8) is

$$(9)\ X\{(\exists c)[(x)((Qx) \equiv (x = c)) \ \& \ (U(c))]\}.$$

An English sentence which might be translated into (9) would be:

(10) George IV wished to know whether one, and only one, individual both wrote *Waverley* and was identical with Scott.

What happens to (2) on the secondary analysis is just that the 'intentional' expression 'George IV wished to know whether' is isolated by the scope operator from the subordinate clause from which the descriptive phrase is to be eliminated. The description is then eliminated from this subordinate proposition exactly as though it had a primary occurrence there. Thus there is really just one analysis of propositions of the form $U(\imath x)(Qx)$, and this is what is conveyed by the definition 14.01. The difference between the primary and the secondary interpretations, as I have been calling them, is determined by the part of (2) (proper or improper) taken as $U(\imath x)(Qx)$. On the secondary interpretation $U(\imath x)(Qx)$ is taken to be not the whole of (2) but the part

(11) Scott is the author of *Waverley*.

Though we have but one analysis of '$U(\imath x)(Qx)$', we have two (non-equivalent) analyses of (2) according as we take the whole of (2) or the part (11) as $U(\imath x)(Qx)$.

4. Let us grant (though it has been disputed) that (11) is correctly analysed by Russell's theory. According to this analysis, it is logically equivalent to

> (12) One and only one individual both wrote *Waverley* and is identical with Scott.

It is assumed that a necessary condition for the correctness of an analysis is that the analysans and the analysandum be logically equivalent. But from the premise that (11) is logically equivalent to (12), it does not follow that (2) under the secondary interpretation (i.e., under the interpretation which sees in it the form (8)) is logically equivalent to some proposition of the form (9), e.g., (10). To argue that since (11) and (12) are logically equivalent, so also are (2) (in the form (8)) and (10) is to argue fallaciously. There is a fallacy in reasoning that since $p$ and $q$ are logically equivalent so are $f(p)$ and $f(q)$ for *any* function of propositions $f$. And we cannot argue thus in this case because (2), under the secondary interpretation, does not express an extensional function of the contained proposition (11). Though it would be fallacious to argue in this way, it does not, of course, follow that (2), thus interpreted, and (10) are not logically equivalent. I want to show that they are not, but I wish first to point out that Russell offers no argument to show that (2) thus interpreted is logically equivalent to (10), although, of course, he does maintain that it is. He argues that (11) and (12) are logically equivalent and does not pursue the matter further. It is for this reason that I suspect that in 'On Denoting' he actually commits the fallacy which I have just warned against.

5. Is (2) (under the secondary interpretation—hereafter this qualification will be omitted) logically equivalent to (10)? It seems to me that it is not. It seems to me that (10) might be false though (2) is true.[1] Asked whether he wants to know whether one, and only one, individual both wrote *Waverley* and is identical

---

[1] Numerals between parentheses are used sometimes as designations of sentences and sometimes as abbreviations. The context resolves this ambiguity.

with Scott, George IV might answer that this is not what he wishes to know, since he *already* knows that one, and only one, individual wrote *Waverley*; what he does not know is whether the author of *Waverley* is Scott. George IV answers thus because he takes it that his interlocutor would not put his question as he does unless assuming that he (George IV) does not know that one, and only one, individual wrote *Waverley*. In this case (2) is true and (10) is not; thus they are not logically equivalent. If this argument is sound it follows that neither the primary nor the secondary interpretation of (2) is correct and that the Theory of Descriptions is incapable of providing an analysis of propositions of the type we are considering. But even if the argument is mistaken the conclusion is correct, for it is true that:

> (13) Linsky argued that it might have been the case that George IV wanted to know whether Scott was the author of *Waverley*, though George IV did not want to know whether one, and only one, individual both wrote *Waverley* and was identical with Scott.

Now (13) is a proposition containing a descriptive phrase, and for reasons already given that phrase cannot be regarded as having a primary occurrence there. But neither can it be regarded as having a secondary occurrence, for on this analysis (13) is logically equivalent to:

> (14) Linsky argued that it might have been the case that George IV wanted to know whether one, and only one, individual both wrote *Waverley*, and was identical with Scott, though George IV did not want to know whether one, and only one, individual both wrote *Waverley* and was identical with Scott.

Though this is not a logical contradiction, it is certainly false and thus not equivalent to (13), which is true. It must be observed that while (14) seems to be the most natural secondary analysis of (13), it is not the only possible one. A secondary analysis of a proposition containing a descriptive phrase is an analysis which eliminates the description from a subordinate propositional part of the whole proposition in which the description occurs. But such a subordinate propositional part of (13) can be selected in seven possible ways. That none of these secondary analyses provides an analysans which is logically equivalent to the analysandum (13) is what is shown in the appendix at the end of this chapter.

6. It has now been established that there are propositions containing descriptive phrases for which any interpretation offered by the Theory of Descriptions is incorrect—incorrect in the sense that the analysans and any analysandum offered by the theory are not logically equivalent. It can also be shown that there are puzzles of essentially the same kind as (1), (2), (3) for which Russell's theory cannot provide a solution, even if (what is not the case) it does supply an adequate treatment of (1), (2), (3). The following is such a 'puzzle'. (1), (13), therefore:

> Linsky argued that it might have been the case that George IV wanted to know whether Scott was Scott, though he did not want to know whether one, and only one, individual both wrote *Waverley* and was identical with Scott.

It is clear that this does not follow from (1) and (13), but the Russellian analysis of (13) into (14) (or into any of the possible alternatives to (14) discussed in the appendix) is incorrect.

The results concerning this example may be generalized. Russell's programme of analysing propositions containing descriptive phrases must fail when the principal verb of the proposition is a verb of propositional attitude ('believes', 'knows', 'supposes', 'wishes to know', etc.). The primary analysis is always incorrect, for on this analysis a proposition containing a descriptive phrase and whose principal verb is a verb of propositional attitude cannot be true unless one, and only one, thing satisfies the description. That such an entailment does not hold for such propositions is part of what Brentano and his followers were trying to express when they expounded their doctrine of 'intentional inexistence'.

Concerning the secondary analysis the situation is somewhat more complicated. In general, the case will be as with (13); more than one secondary analysis is possible. But each such analysis will produce an analysans which falls into one of two classes of cases. The analysans may (like $(13d^{d'})$ of the appendix) have the same objectionable feature as that produced by the primary analysis, i.e., the existence of the described object is entailed by the analysans. This will be the case when the propositional part from which the description is eliminated itself contains the verb of propositional attitude which is the principal verb of the whole proposition in which the description is taken to have secondary occurrence. Or, on the other hand, the secondary analysis may eliminate the descriptive phrase from some subordinate propositional part which does not contain the principal verb of the whole proposition containing that part. This subordinate propositional part will be within the scope of the verb of propositional attitude. Since Russell's analysis of propositions containing descriptive phrases provides an analysans which is logically equivalent but not synonymous with its analysandum, we are required, by Russell's programme in this latter type of case, to replace a proposition under the scope of a verb of propositional attitude by another proposition which is logically equivalent but not synonymous with it. Under this replacement logical equivalence is not preserved, for what we have done is to replace a proposition by another logically equivalent one within the scope of a non-extensional propositional operator. This, we know, is not a valid mode of inference. This failure is particularly interesting because it reveals how closely Russell's programme of analysis is tied to the extensional point of view.

7. The distinction between the primary and the secondary interpretations of propositions whose principal verb is a verb of propositional attitude is useful in introducing another important consideration concerning these words. Verbs of propositional attitude, non-extensional concepts generally, are, in a certain sense, Janus-faced. One of their faces is extensional (or transparent); the other face is intensional (or 'opaque', as Quine uses this term). Intensional propositions are, in general, ambiguous. They can be understood opaquely, and they can be understood transparently. Suppose I say, 'Oedipus wanted to marry his mother.' Understood opaquely, what I have said is wildly false. But it can be understood transparently, and so understood, it is true. Oedipus did want to marry his mother, since he wanted to marry Jocasta. And who was Jocasta? His mother! Understood transparently, 'Oedipus wanted to marry his mother' means something like, 'Oedipus wanted to marry a person who, in fact, was his mother'. This last would naturally be understood not to imply that Oedipus knew that the woman he wanted to marry was,

in fact, his mother. Understood opaquely, 'Oedipus wanted to marry his mother' means something like 'Oedipus desired to make true the proposition that the mother of Oedipus is the wife of Oedipus'. This last paraphrase is correct only if it would naturally be understood in such a way that it would not be true unless Oedipus did know that the woman he wanted to marry was his mother. Certainly in the case of the proposition we are considering ('Oedipus wanted to marry his mother') the opaque interpretation is the more natural one, and that is why it strikes one, straight off, as wildly false. But one can understand these words transparently, and thus they exemplify my thesis, viz., that propositions whose principal verb is a verb of propositional attitude are, in the way indicated, ambiguous.

How is all of this related to Russell's distinction between the primary and the secondary interpretations of propositions containing descriptive phrases? It seems to me that Russell was aware of the ambiguity which I have attempted to bring out. There is reason to suppose that he believed that the distinction between the primary and secondary interpretation of propositions (which like (2)) have a verb of propositional attitude as their main verb, corresponds to the distinction between their transparent and their opaque interpretations. There is reason to suppose that Russell believed that his primary interpretation gives a correct analysis of such propositions transparently understood, and that his secondary analysis gives a correct analysis of these propositions opaquely understood.

If Russell did believe these things, then I think that he was partly right and partly wrong. He was right if he thought that his primary analysis was correct for propositions expressing propositional attitudes when these latter are transparently understood. Let us see how this works out for (2). Suppose that George IV sees Scott dimly in the distance through a thick English fog. He wonders who it is and makes a guess. He asks, 'Is that man possibly Scott?' It seems to me that it would be perfectly correct to report this incident by saying 'George IV wished to know whether Scott was Scott'. The words *might* mislead an audience, but if the situation were entirely clear to that audience there is no reason, as far as I can see, for saying that the report is false. The incident might equally correctly be reported in these words: 'George IV wished to know, concerning the man who had in fact written *Waverley*, whether he was Scott', or again 'One and only one individual both wrote *Waverley* and was such that George IV wanted to know whether he was Scott'. Now both of these last two say what, on Russell's analysis, is said by (2) on the primary analysis. I believe that they give possible interpretations of (2), though certainly these interpretations are not the natural ones. Notice that if this interpretation is taken (1), (2), (3) is a valid argument. This alone brings out how unnatural the primary interpretation is.

But I have also argued that Russell was partly wrong. He was wrong if he thought that his secondary analysis was correct for propositions expressing propositional attitudes opaquely understood. This is what I have been trying to demonstrate in Sections 5 and 6 of this chapter. But it should be clear that this failure concerns only the opaque interpretations of the propositions in question ((2), (13)). It is also clear that Russell understands (2) opaquely, for understood transparently (1), (2), (3) is (as I have shown) a valid argument, and Russell assumes from the beginning, as we all naturally do, that the argument is invalid. The two terms of a true identity statement can replace each other, *salva veritate*, even in positions governed by verbs of propositional attitude, so long as these verbs are transparently understood. That such substitution is a valid mode of inference for a given context is often cited as a mark of extensionality. Looked at in this way, we can see how Russell's programme of analysis is, in another way, tied to the extensional point of view. We can say that his analysis of propositions expressing propositional attitudes is correct as long as these propositions are interpreted extensionally.

8. (2), under the secondary interpretation, has been represented as having the form (8). There is something misleading about thus representing it, and when this has been shown we will be in a position to see that there is a disparity between the treatment of descriptions in 'On Denoting' and their treatment in Chapter XIV of *Principia Mathematica*. When (2) is given the secondary interpretation (1), (2), (3) is valid if, and only if, (15) is valid.

$$(15) \ \{a = (\imath x)(Qx)\} \supset \{X[\imath x)(Qx)][U(\imath x)(Qx)] \supset [X(U(a))]\}.$$

In the final paragraph of Chapter XIV of *Principia* Russell says,

'It should be observed that the proposition in which $(\imath x)(Qx)$ has the larger scope always implies the corresponding one in which it has the smaller scope, but the converse implication only holds if either (a) we have $E!(\imath x)(Qx)$ or (b) the proposition in which $(\imath x)(Qx)$ has the smaller scope implies $E!(\imath x)(Qx)$.' Part of what Russell is here telling us is put formally thus:

$$(16)\ \{E!(\imath x)(Qx)\} \supset [\{X[(\imath x)(Qx)]U(\imath x)(Qx)\} \equiv \{[(\imath x)(Qx)]X(U(\imath x)(Qx))\}].$$

Now if this is true, the interpretation which accords a secondary occurrence to 'the author of *Waverley*' in (2) will yield an argument (call it '(1'), (2'), (3')') which is valid. This can be shown as follows. (1), (2), (3) is valid when the descriptive phrase is accorded a primary occurrence in (2), i.e., the following is valid:

$$1.\quad a = (\imath x)(Qx)$$
$$2.\quad X(U(\imath x)(Qx))$$

$$\overline{\qquad\qquad\qquad\qquad}$$

$$3.\ \therefore X(U(a))$$

What we want to show is that the argument which accords a secondary occurrence to the description is also valid.

$$(1')\quad a = (\imath x)(Qx)$$
$$(2')\quad X[(\imath x)(Qx)]U(\imath x)(Qx)$$

$$\overline{\qquad\qquad\qquad\qquad}$$

$$(3').\ : X(U(a))$$

Now it is valid for from (1') follows (4') $E!(\imath x)(Qx)$ (by 14.21). By assumption we have (5')

$$\{E!(\imath x)(Qx)\} \supset [\{X[(\imath x)(Qx)]U(\imath x)(Qx)\} \equiv \{[(\imath x)(Qx)]X(U(\imath x)(Qx))\}]$$

Hence from (4') and (5') and *modus ponens* we get

$$(6')\ \{X[(\imath x)(Qx)]U(\imath x)(Qx)\} \equiv \{[(\imath x)(Qx)]X(U(\imath x)(Qx))\}.$$

Now by (2') and (6') and *modus ponens* (first dissolving the biconditional) we get

$$(7')\ [(\imath x)(Qx)]X(U(\imath x)(Qx)).$$

But (7') = 2, and (1') = 1, hence since 1, 2, 3 is valid and (3') = 3, it follows that (3').

Russell thought the argument was invalid; and so it is. The source of the difficulty is that (16) is not true. Russell says that (16) is true in at least three places in *Principia*. In the Introduction (p. 70) he says, 'It will be seen further that when $E!(\imath x)(Qx)$, we may enlarge or diminish the scope of $(\imath x)(Qx)$ as much as we please without altering the truth-value of any proposition in which it occurs.' Again in Chapter XIV (p. 185) he says, 'The purpose of the following propositions is to show that when $E!(\imath x)(Qx)$, the scope of $(\imath x)(Qx)$ does not matter to the truth-value of any proposition in which $(\imath x)(Qx)$ occurs. This proposition cannot be proved generally, but it can be proved in each particular case.' We are then given a series of theorems (14.31 to 14.34), in which it is proven that when $(\imath x)(Qx)$ occurs in the form $X(\imath x)(Qx)$ and $X(\imath x)(Qx)$ occurs in a larger proposition built out of it, the scope of $(\imath x)(Qx)$ does not affect the truth-value of the larger proposition, provided $E!(\imath x)(Qx)$.

But, though this principle (16) is not true, there is a theorem corresponding to it which says that when $X(\imath x)(Qx)$ occurs in a larger proposition built up *truth-functionally* out of it, the scope of $(\imath x)(Qx)$ does not affect the truth-value of the larger proposition, provided $E!(\imath x)(Qx)$.

$$14.3 \; \{[(p \equiv q) \supset {}_{p,q}(f(p) \equiv f(q))] \; \& \; E!(\imath x)(Qx)\} \supset$$
$$[f\{[(\imath x)(Qx)]X(\imath x)(Qx)\}] \equiv [[(\imath x)(Qx)]f\{X(\imath x)(Qx)\}]$$

But *this* theorem cannot be used, as was (16) to establish the validity of (1'), (2'), (3') because (2') is not a truth-function of $U(\imath x)(Qx)$.

9. What (16) says is that provided $E!(\imath x)(Qx)$, the proposition giving the larger scope to $(\imath x)(Qx)$, i.e., giving it primary occurrence, is equivalent to the proposition giving it the smaller scope, i.e., secondary occurrence. This is true provided extensional functions only are involved. Thus 14.3. I do not wish to suggest that Russell believed (16) also to hold for non-extensional functions. For this reason the reduction of (1'), (2'), (3') to 1, 2, 3 carried out above is mistaken, and once again we escape the conclusion that our argument is valid. But we also see what is misleading about the view which sees in (2) a proposition of the form (8), for if the logic of the theory of descriptions does not apply to (2) because of its non-extensional character, how can (2)

have the logical form of a formula of the theory? (8) can be no more than mere shorthand for (2), it cannot display its logical form. What, then, do we finally learn is the mistake in (1), (2), (3)? We learn that the analysis offered by the Theory of Descriptions does not apply to the proposition (2). There is no problem in (1), (2), (3) of confusing proper names with descriptive phrases. The fault lies with the so-called principle of the substitutivity of identicals. It does not hold for non-extensional contexts.

10. It is not difficult, I believe, to see why this false principle was accepted. It was accepted because it was not distinguished from another principle, i.e., the principle of the indiscernibility of identicals. This principle states that if $x = y$, then any property of $x$ is a property of $y$, and conversely. But this is not at all to say what the principle of the substitutivity of identicals says, viz., that if $a$ and $b$ are names (or other designations) for the same thing, then $a$ can replace $b$ in any true proposition in which it occurs (and conversely $b$ can replace $a$) *salva veritate*.

We can see the confusion of these two principles in Russell's formulation of the principle of substitutivity. 'If $a$ is identical with $b$, whatever is true of the one is true of the other, and either may be substituted for the other in any proposition without altering the truth or falsehood of that proposition.' It is true that if $a$ is identical with $b$, whatever is true of the one is true of the other, if this means that every property of $a$ is a property of $b$ and conversely. Russell then goes on to say, '. . . and either may be substituted for the other in any proposition', *salva veritate*. But what we substitute in a proposition is not $a$ for $b$ (or conversely) but names (or other designations) for $a$ and $b$. So if we correct the use–mention confusion in this formulation we obtain the following principle: 'If $a$ is identical with $b$, whatever is true of the one is true of the other, and names (or other designations) for $a$ and $b$ may be substituted for each other in any proposition *salva veritate*.' But this principle is false, as is evidenced by (1), (2), (3). The assumption which makes it seem that we must accept this false principle is the assumption that any open sentence expresses a property. If this assumption were correct, then the (corrected) principle of substitutivity would be entailed by the principle of the indiscernibility of identicals. But we have only to state this assumption to see that it is dubious.

To leave the matter here is clearly unsatisfactory. Some open sentences do express properties. Which do and which do not? I do not know how to draw this line, nor so far as I know, does anybody else. To that extent it still remains a problem as to what is wrong with (1), (2), (3).[1]

[1] Some of the things said here about the relation of the principle of substitutivity to the principle of the indiscernibility of identicals are taken from an unpublished paper by Richard L. Cartwright. This chapter was published in a slightly different form in the *Journal of Philosophy*, 1966, pp. 673–83.

# APPENDIX

It has been argued in this chapter that Russell's analysis of the proposition (13) is incorrect in the sense that the analysans which it provides is not logically equivalent (hereafter, 'L-equivalent') to the analysandum. The argument against the primary analysis is presented in section 3 of this chapter, and part of the argument against the secondary analysis is presented in section 5. That discussion in section 5 is supplemented and completed in this appendix. When a descriptive phrase has secondary occurrence in a proposition it must be eliminated from a subordinate propositional part of the whole proposition in which it occurs. Thus, in general, there will be more than one such secondary interpretation. There will be as many secondary interpretations as there are relevant subordinate propositional parts. In the case of proposition (13), seven such cases are to be considered. What we must show is that none of the propositions resulting from the elimination of the descriptive phrase from (13) is L-equivalent to the original. In section 5 we have shown that this is the case for only one of the possible alternatives. It was the alternative which, in some sense, it is most natural to choose. In this appendix all of the alternatives will be discussed, however unlikely they may seem as possible interpretations of (13). In order of length the parts of (13) to be considered are the following:

(*a*) Scott was the author of *Waverley*.

(*b*) George IV wanted to know whether Scott was the author of *Waverley*.

(*c*) It might have been the case that George IV wanted to know whether Scott was the author of *Waverley*.

(*d*) Linsky argued that it might have been the case that George IV wanted to know whether Scott was the author of *Waverley*.

(*e*) Scott was the author of *Waverley*, though George IV did not want to know whether one, and only one, individual both wrote *Waverley* and was identical with Scott.

(*f*) George IV wanted to know whether Scott was the author of *Waverley*, though George IV did not want to know whether one, and only one, individual both wrote *Waverley* and was identical with Scott.

(*g*) It might have been the case that George IV wanted to know whether Scott was the author of *Waverley*, though George IV did not want to know whether one, and only one, individual both wrote *Waverley* and was identical with Scott.

In order to determine the secondary interpretations of (13) we proceed as follows. We extract each of the seven subordinate propositions (*a*)–(*g*) one at a time from (13). We eliminate the descriptive phrase from each of these obtaining the propositions (*a'*), (*b'*), (*c'*), (*d'*), (*e'*), (*f'*), (*g'*). We now insert each of (*a'*)–(*g'*) into the position resulting from the extraction. We thus obtain the seven possible secondary analyses of (13). First, then, we present the propositions (*a'*)–(*g'*) which result from elimination of the descriptive phrase from the propositions (*a*)–(*g*).

(*a'*) One, and only one, individual both wrote *Waverley* and was identical with Scott.

(*b'*) One, and only one, individual both wrote *Waverley* and was such that George IV wanted to know whether he was Scott.

(*c'*) One, and only one, individual both wrote *Waverley* and was such that it might have been the case that George IV wanted to know whether he was Scott.

(*d'*) One, and only one, individual both wrote *Waverley* and was such that Linsky argued that it might have been the case that George IV wanted to know whether he was Scott.

(*e'*) One, and only one, individual both wrote *Waverley* and was such that though George IV did not want to know whether one, and only one, individual both wrote *Waverley* and was identical with Scott, he was identical with Scott.

(*f'*) One, and only one, individual both wrote *Waverley* and was such that though George IV did not want to know whether one, and only one, individual both wrote *Waverley* and was identical with Scott, George IV wanted to know whether he was identical with Scott.

($g'$) One, and only one, individual both wrote *Waverley* and was such that though George IV did not want to know whether one, and only one, individual both wrote *Waverley* and was identical with Scott, it might have been the case that George IV wanted to know whether he was identical with Scott.

Now the next step is to insert ($a'$) into (13) in place of ($a$); ($b'$) into (13) in place of ($b$); and so on for each of ($a'$)–($g'$) and ($a$)–($g$). The result, I maintain, is that in each case we obtain a proposition not L-equivalent to the original. First then we replace ($a$) in (13) by ($a'$), the result is

13($a^{a'}$) Linsky argued that it might have been the case that George IV wanted to know whether one, and only one, individual both wrote *Waverley* and was identical with Scott, though George IV did not want to know whether one, and only one, individual both wrote *Waverley* and was identical with Scott.

Clearly (13) and (13$a^{a'}$) are not L-equivalent. (13$a^{a'}$) though not a logical contradiction is certainly false, and thus not equivalent to (13). (13$a^{a'}$) is the same as (14) discussed in the body of this chapter.

Next let us replace ($b$) by ($b'$) in (13) to obtain

(13$b^{b'}$) Linsky argued that it might have been the case that one, and only one, individual both wrote *Waverley* and was such that George IV wanted to know whether he was Scott, though George IV did not want to know whether one, and only one, individual both wrote *Waverley* and was identical with Scott.

(13$b^{b'}$) is again false, and so not L-equivalent to (13). The remaining alternatives are presented below without further comment. In each case the reader can convince himself that they are not L-equivalent to (13). The last three alternatives are difficult to understand. All of these are to be understood opaquely, as is the original (13). The following suggestion will help the reader to see the sense of the last three alternatives. Treat the words 'though George IV did not want to know whether one, and only one, individual both wrote *Waverley* and was identical with Scott', which occur in each of them as a parenthetical clause interrupting the sense of the remainder of the sentence. Notice that $(13a^{d'})$ suffers from the same difficulty as the primary interpretation as a possible analysis of $(13)$, it implies that *Waverley* was not co-authored.

$(13c^{c'})$ Linsky argued that one, and only one, individual both wrote *Waverley* and was such that it might have been the case that George IV wanted to know whether he was Scott, though George IV did not want to know whether one, and only one, individual both wrote *Waverley* and was identical with Scott.

$(13c^{c'})$ is not L-equivalent with $(13)$, and so for $(13a^{d'})$, $(13e^{e'})$, $(13f^{f'})$, and $(13g^{g'})$. These will, for completeness, here be recorded.

$(13a^{d'})$ One, and only one, individual both wrote *Waverley* and was such that Linsky argued that it might have been the case that George IV wanted to know whether he was Scott, though George IV did not want to know whether one, and only one, individual both wrote *Waverley* and was identical with Scott.

$(13e^{e'})$ Linsky argued that it might have been the case that George IV wanted to know whether one, and only one, individual both wrote *Waverley* and was such that though George IV did not want to know whether one, and only one, individual both wrote *Waverley* and was identical with Scott, he was identical with Scott.

$(13f^{f'})$ Linsky argued that it might have been the case that one, and only one, individual both wrote *Waverley* and was such that though George IV did not want to know whether one, and only one, individual both wrote *Waverley* and was identical with Scott, George IV wanted to know whether he was identical with Scott.

$(13g^{g'})$ Linsky argued that one, and only one, individual both wrote *Waverley* and was such that though George IV did not want to know whether one, and only one, individual both wrote *Waverley* and was identical with Scott, it might have been the case that George IV wanted to know whether he was identical with Scott.

# VI
## STRAWSON ON REFERRING

1. With Strawson the study of definite descriptions becomes part of a broader topic, referring. Descriptions are but one of a large class of expressions characteristically used in a 'uniquely referring way', i.e., 'to mention or refer to some individual person or single object or particular event or place or process in the course of doing what we should normally describe as making a statement about that person, object, place, event, or process'.[1] The class of expressions to be studied includes 'singular demonstrative pronouns ("this" and "that"); proper names (e.g. "Venice", "Napoleon", "John"); singular personal and impersonal pronouns ("he", "she", "I", "you", "it"); and phrases beginning with the definite article followed by a noun, qualified or unqualified, in the singular (e.g., "the table", "the old man", "the king of France").'[2] This is the class of expressions which can occur as the subject of a subject–predicate sentence. When so occurring they exemplify the 'uniquely referring use'.

We have entered different terrain from that occupied by Russell. This is conspicuously marked by the prevalence, in Strawson's discussions, of the word 'use'. Russell's aim is the analysis of a certain class of propositions; Strawson's aim is to study a certain use of words. This divergence is important. Because of it, this controversy takes on a character found so often in major philosophical disputes. What at first looks like a clash of contradictory views about the same subject turns out to be a statement of compatible views about different subjects. This is not all that is involved in this dispute. Some of Strawson's criticisms hit their

---

[1] 'On Referring', reprinted in *Essays in Philosophical Analysis*, ed. by A. G. N. Flew, Macmillan Co., London, 1956, p. 21.
[2] *Ibid.*, p. 21. All quotations from Strawson in this chapter are taken from this source, unless otherwise indicated by footnotes.

mark and are correct. But many important ones do not. Either they are wrong or it can be shown that what Strawson regards as criticisms of Russell's views are really compatible with them. It is the 'uniquely referring use' of some words and only secondarily these words themselves which concerns Strawson. The same words may have various uses. For example, the words 'the whale' in the sentence 'The whale is a mammal' (uttered, say, in a biology class) have a different use from the one they have in the sentence 'The whale struck the ship' (uttered with the aim of informing us of our plight). The second use is a uniquely referring one. The first is not. A consequence of this concern with the use of words is that considerations become relevant in Strawson's theory which had no place in Russell's; considerations concerning the users of language, and the situations, contexts, and circumstances in which words are used.

2. Strawson launches his attack immediately. 'I think it is true to say that Russell's Theory of Descriptions, which is concerned with the last of the four classes of expressions I mentioned above (i.e., with expressions of the form "the so-and-so"), is still widely accepted among logicians as giving a correct account of the use of such expressions in ordinary language. I want to show in the first place, that this theory, so regarded, embodies some fundamental mistakes.' Suppose someone were now seriously to utter the sentence 'The king of France is wise'. The sentence is not meaningless. But there is not at present a king of France. How can the sentence not be meaningless when there is nothing which answers to the description 'The king of France'? One of the objectives of the Theory of Descriptions was to provide an answer to this question which would enable us to avoid another answer which Russell found objectionable, viz., that of Meinong.

Let us consider Strawson's version of Russell's solution of this difficulty. For convenience let $S$ represent the sentence 'The king of France is wise', and let $D$ represent the phrase 'The king of France'.[1] 'The mistake arises, he [Russell] says, from thinking that $D$, which is certainly the *grammatical* subject of $S$, is also the *logical* subject of $S$. But $D$ is not the logical subject of $S$. In fact, $S$, although grammatically it has a singular subject and predicate,

---

[1] These letters function both as designations of the expressions in question and as abbreviations for them. The context resolves this ambiguity.

is not logically a subject–predicate sentence at all. The proposition it expresses is a complex kind of *existential* proposition, part of which might be described as a "uniquely existential" proposition'.

Now, according to Strawson, Russell could only have thought that these observations cleared up the difficulty about *S* if he were making certain false assumptions. What Russell is falsely assuming is that if a sentence is logically of the subject–predicate form, 'then the very fact of its being significant, having a meaning guarantees that there *is* something referred to by the logical (and grammatical subject)'.

Strawson objects to this assumption, though it seems perfectly correct to me. Apparently he thinks that a sentence can be of the subject–predicate form even when it is not the case that something is referred to by the grammatical subject, and presumably he thinks that *S* provides an example. But this is a mistake. According to my dictionary, a subject, in the grammatical sense, is just 'The word or group of words denoting that of which anything is affirmed or predicated'. According to my dictionary, then, there just cannot be such a thing as a grammatical subject which does not denote (or refer to) anything; that (by definition) is what the subject of a sentence does. Surely the subject of *S*, viz., *D*, does denote (in the sense of the dictionary) something—the king of France. But to say that the subject of *S* denotes the king of France is not the same as to say that there is such a thing as a king of France. It is Strawson's confusion at this point which accounts for his view that there may be nothing denoted by the grammatical subject of a sentence.

Let us make this correction. Now Strawson's criticism comes to this. Russell assumes that *S* cannot be a meaningful sentence unless either it is not really of the subject–predicate form or there is a king of France. That is, Russell assumes that if *S* is logically of the subject–predicate form there is a king of France. The reason is that he holds that a sentence can only be logically of the subject–predicate form if its subject is a genuine proper name, and he holds that a genuine proper name can only name something which exists. Russell holds this latter view because he thinks that the meaning of a name is just its bearer. Now if one holds these views one is committed to saying what Russell does about *S*. For if *S* is logically of the subject–predicate form the subject term of *S* is a proper name. Since the meaning of a proper name is assumed

to be the bearer of the name, and since there is no such thing as
*D*, it follows that if *S* is of the subject–predicate form it is meaningless, since it would then contain a meaningless constituent.
But since *S* is not meaningless, Russell concluded that *S* is not
genuinely of the subject–predicate form. What he should have
concluded is that the bearer of a name is not to be confused with
the meaning (if any) of the name. It was Wittgenstein who made
this criticism first. Strawson is in agreement with Wittgenstein
here, and it seems to me that both of them are correct as against
Russell.

3. In order to present his criticisms of Russell's theory, Strawson
introduces two parallel triples of distinctions applicable to sentences and expressions. By 'expression' is meant an expression
which has a 'uniquely referring use' and by a 'sentence' is meant a
sentence beginning with such an expression. The distinctions are
between:

($A$1) a sentence,
($A$2) a use of a sentence,
($A$3) an utterance of a sentence,

and, correspondingly, between:

($B$1) an expression,
($B$2) a use of an expression,
($B$3) an utterance of an expression.

Now let us consider the sentence 'The king of France is wise'.
We can imagine it being spoken on various occasions from the
beginning of the seventeenth century onwards. Notice first that
we are using the word 'sentence' in the sense of sentence-type
rather than sentence-token, since we have spoken of one and the
same sentence being spoken on several occasions. If one man had
uttered our sentence in the reign of Louis XIV and another man
had uttered it in the reign of Louis XV they would have been
talking about different people, and it would be natural to say that
they had made different assertions, since one might hold that the
first assertion was true and the second false. But if two men had
uttered these words, both in the reign of Louis XIV, then either
both men made a true assertion or both men made a false assertion.
Now this illustrates what is meant by ($A$2). We could say of the

first two men that they made different uses of the same sentence, and we could say of the second two men that they made the same use of the sentence. Of course, in another sense, all of our men have made the same use of the sentence since they have all used it to make an assertion rather than say, as an example in the teaching of English, or non-'seriously' in some way, e.g., on the stage.

Similarly for the B-distinctions. Just as the sentence 'The king of France is wise' can be used to make different assertions, or none at all, so the expression 'The king of France' can be used to refer to different people on different occasions of its use.

> Generally, as against Russell, I shall say this [says Strawson]. Meaning (in at least one important sense) is a function of the sentence or expression; mentioning and referring and truth or falsity are functions of the use of the sentence or expression. To give the meaning of an expression (in the sense in which I am using the word) is to give *general directions* for its use in making true or false assertions. It is not to talk about any particular occasion of the use of the sentence or expression. The meaning of an expression cannot be identified with the object it is used, on a particular occasion to refer to. The meaning of a sentence cannot be identified with the assertion it is used, on a particular occasion, to make. For to talk about the meaning of an expression or sentence is not to talk about its use on a particular occasion, but about the rules, habits, conventions, governing its correct use, on all occasions to refer or to assert.

By confusing assertions (or statements) with sentences and their uses, Russell made the mistake of thinking that anyone now uttering the sentence 'The king of France is wise', would be making either a true or a false assertion. According to Strawson, there is a third possibility, viz., that someone now uttering these words would be saying something which is neither true nor false. Russell rejected this possibility because he held that the alternative to being true or false was to be nonsense. Strawson holds that Russell makes this mistake because he fails to notice the distinctions indicated above. It is statements (or assertions) that are true or false, not sentences, and it is a sentence that is significant or meaningless, not a statement. Thus the sentence $S$ can be significant, though on a particular occasion of its use no statement (true or false) is made by the use of this sentence. This is Russell's principal error. He thinks that the only alternative to saying something true or false when we utter $S$ is that $S$ should not be significant at all. And he makes this mistake because he does not distinguish sentences from statements.

4. Strawson's main objection to the Theory of Descriptions can be stated in terms of Russell's analysis of the statement 'The king of France is wise'. According to Russell, this entails 'There is one, and only one, king of France'. We have called the former of these statements $S$, let us call the latter $S'$. Strawson's contention is that Russell has misconceived the true character of the relation which holds between $S$ and $S'$. As opposed to Russell's view that $S$ entails $S'$, Strawson holds that $S$ presupposes $S'$. What this means is that if $S$ is either true or false (has a truth-value) $S'$ must be true. In other words, it is a necessary condition for $S$ to have a truth-value (true or false) that $S'$ be true. In still other words, Strawson maintains that:

$S$ is true or false, entails that $S'$ is true. [1]

Strawson's reason for preferring his own account over that given by Russell is this. Since $S'$ is false, if we accept Russell's account, we must conclude by *modus tollens*, that $S$ is false. But this is wrong, according to Strawson. He says:

> Now suppose someone were in fact to say to you with a perfectly serious air: 'The king of France is wise'. Would you say, 'That's untrue'? I think it is quite certain that you would not. But suppose he went on to *ask* you whether you thought that what he had just said was true, or was false; whether you agreed or disagreed with what he had just said. I think you would be inclined, with some hesitation, to say that you did not do either; that the question of whether his statement was true or false simply *did not arise*, because there was no such person as the king of France.

5. It seems to me that Strawson has stated his views in a way which is misleading as to the true nature and extent of his disagreement with Russell. Russell's theory is concerned with the analysis of a certain class of propositions, while Strawson's account is a theory about statements. Strawson does not discuss the difference between statements and propositions. He even, at times, writes as though there were no important differences be-

[1] *Introduction to Logical Theory*, Methuen & Co., London, 1952, p. 175.

tween statements, assertions, and propositions. Of course, there
is a great deal which needs clarification in the notion of a proposition; but one point is clear about them, and this happens to
be crucial in the present context. As logicians and logical theorists
employ the term 'proposition', every proposition is either true or
false. Since statements can be truth-valueless, it follows that the
concept of a statement is different from the concept of a proposition.

So far as the logic of the situation is concerned, it would be
open to Russell to say the following in reply to Strawson,

> I agree with all your observations about statements. I agree that
> the statement that the king of France is wise is truth-valueless. But
> the proposition that the king of France is wise cannot, by definition,
> be truth-valueless. And you have given no argument whatever to
> show that the proposition that the king of France is wise does not
> entail the proposition that there is one and only one king of France.

Perhaps an analogy with geometry will be of help here. We
must distinguish between the formal calculus of (say) Euclidean
geometry, the geometrical objects (circles, planes, lines, points)
which are the values of the variables of this calculus, and physical
or spatial objects corresponding to these geometrical ones, the
triangle on the blackboard, the rectangle formed by the building
blocks for the foundation of a house. Now, of course, no one
refutes Euclidean geometry by pointing out that the triangle on
the blackboard has an angle sum of more than 180° when measured
with the most accurate instruments. Similarly, we must distinguish
between the logical calculus, the propositions which are the values
of its variables and the utterances, sayings, or statements which
people produce in their everyday use of language. Just as geometry remains unrefuted by measurements of physical triangles,
so logic is not refuted by the discovery that there are statements
which we would not call either true or false, but (say) exaggerated,
or vague, or inaccurate. But this is exactly what Strawson does
when he criticizes Russellian logic.

6. Strawson is not consistent in this procedure. For the most part
he accepts classical and modern logic as accurately presenting the
logical relations holding between statements. It is only with
Russell's Theory of Descriptions that he finds fault. He even

accepts the traditional square of opposition, rejecting the Russellian criticisms. But in the course of rejecting Russell's criticisms of the traditional square, and elsewhere in his book, *Introduction to Logical Theory*, he produces arguments which are inconsistent with the arguments which he employs against the Theory of Descriptions. This inconsistency is remarkable because the difficulties which Russell found with the traditional square are practically identical with those which Strawson finds in Russell's Theory of Descriptions. Both sets of difficulties concern what might be called (though mistakenly) 'nondenoting subject terms'.

These difficulties are too well known in the case of the square for it to be necessary for us to state them here. Let us consider Strawson's resolution of them and his rehabilitation of the square. It is necessary to quote Strawson in full.

> What I am proposing, then, is this. There are many ordinary sentences beginning with such phrases as 'all . . .', 'all the . . .', 'no . . .', 'none of the . . .', 'some . . .', 'some of the . . .', 'at least one . . .', 'at least one of the . . .' which exhibit, in their standard employment, parallel characteristics to those I have just described in the case of a representative 'all . . .' sentence. That is to say, the existence of members of the subject class is to be regarded as presupposed (in the special sense described) by statements made by the use of these sentences; to be regarded as a necessary condition, not of the truth simply, but of the truth or falsity, of such statements. I am proposing that the four Aristotelian forms should be interpreted as forms of statement of this kind. Will the adoption of this proposal protect the system from the charge of being inconsistent when interpreted? Obviously it will. For every case of invalidity, of breakdown in the laws, arose from the non-existence of members of some subject class being compatible with the truth, or with the falsity, of some statement of one of the four forms. So our proposal, which makes the non-existence of members of the subject class incompatible with either the truth or falsity of any statement of these forms, will cure all these troubles at one stroke. We are to imagine that every logical rule of the system, when expressed in terms of truth and falsity, is preceded by the phrase 'assuming that the statements concerned are either true or false, then . . .' Thus the rule that *A* is the contradictory of *O* states that, *if corresponding statements of the A and O forms both have truth-values*, then they must have opposite truth-values; the rule that *A* entails *I* states that, *if corresponding statements of these forms have truth-values*, then if the statement of the *A* form is true, the statement of the *I* form must be

true; and so on. The suggestion that entailment-rules should be understood in this way is not peculiar to the present case.[1]

In this last sentence Strawson is referring to his treatment of the system of truth-functional connectives. The tables which he presents are identical with those found for the definitions of the connectives in standard treatments of truth-functional logic. After presenting them Strawson imagines an objector who says, 'But what guarantees that there is just this number of possibilities in each case? Do we not speak of half-truths, are we not inclined, sometimes, with all the facts before us, to hesitate to call a statement either true or false; or perhaps, inclined to call it both.'[2] Strawson's reply here is to say exactly what he says in dealing with the square of opposition. We are not to understand these tables as denying that there are other possibilities for statements beside being true or false. We understand them as saying that if (and only if) the statements which go to form a truth-functional compound have truth-values (are either true or false), then the compound has the truth-value assigned to it by the tables.

But now we can return to the inconsistency mentioned at the beginning of this section, for the same technique which is employed by Strawson to overcome the difficulty with the truth-tables and Russell's criticisms of the square dissolves some of his own criticisms of Russell's Theory of Descriptions. If the argument is sound in the one case it is sound in the other, and if it is unsound in the one case it is unsound in the other. How does this work?

We can imagine someone (Strawson) making this objection to Russell's Theory of Descriptions. '$S$ does not entail $S'$, for since $S'$ is false, it follows from Russell's theory by *modus tollens* that $S$ is false. But $S$ is not false, rather it is truth-valueless. Therefore we cannot accept Russell's theory according to which $S$ entails $S'$.' The answer to this is exactly what Strawson says in the case of the similar difficulty over 'non-denoting' subject terms in the square. He must, to be consistent, understand the entailments maintained in the Theory of Descriptions in the following way. When it is said that $S$ entails $S'$ this means that *if $S$ and $S'$ have truth-values, then, necessarily, if $S$ is true, so is $S'$*. This definition is perfectly

---

[1] *Introduction to Logical Theory*, Methuen & Co., London, 1952, pp. 176-7.
[2] *Ibid.*, pp. 68-9.

compatible with its being the case both that $S$ is, as Strawson says, truth-valueless and that, as Russell says, $S$ entails $S'$.

On this understanding of what is asserted by the theory of descriptions, we cannot conclude, as Strawson feared, that since $S$ entails $S'$ and $S'$ is false that $S$ is false. What we can conclude from these premises is that either $S$ is false or it is truth-valueless. And this conclusion is, of course, compatible with Strawson's view that $S$ is truth-valueless.

7. What we have shown so far is that on Strawson's account of entailment, his view that $S$ is truth-valueless is compatible with the theory he is attempting to refute. It can now be shown that his view that $S$ presupposes $S'$, on his account of entailment, entails that $S$ entails $S'$, i.e., these views of Strawson together entail that feature of Russell's theory to which he most strongly objects. The argument is as follows. Let us assume that $S$ presupposes $S'$. What this means is that from the premise that $S$ has a truth-value, it follows that $S'$ is true. But if $S$ is true, it follows that $S$ has a truth-value. Therefore, if $S$ is true, it follows that $S'$ is true. But $S$ is true if, and only if, the king of France is wise, and $S'$ is true if, and only if, one, and only one, person is king of France. Therefore the statement that the king of France is wise entails the statement that one, and only one, person is king of France.

Now it might be objected to this argument that there is a step in it which Strawson would reject. This is the step which says '$S$ is true if, and only if, the king of France is wise, and $S'$ is true if, and only if, one, and only one, person is king of France'. Let us call these equivalences 'Tarski equivalences'.[1] It might be thought that Strawson could argue against the first Tarski equivalence as follows. ' "$S$ is true" is not logically equivalent to "The king of France is wise" because though if "$S$ is true" is true, "The king of France is wise" must also be true, still if "$S$ is true" is false, it does not follow that "The king of France is wise" is false. For the latter may be (and is) truth-valueless.' Thus it is possible for '$S$ is true' to be false when 'The king of France is wise' is not false, so the first Tarski equivalence must be rejected. A similar argument would require us to reject the second Tarski equivalence.

[1] Cf. 'The Semantic Conception of Truth', reprinted in *Semantics and the Philosophy of Language*, (ed.) by L. Linsky, University of Illinois Press, Urbana, 1952.

But this argument is not available to Strawson. Strawson could not use it without violating his own account of the biconditional. On that account, the result of joining two statements by the biconditional connective is a true statement if, and only if, the statements joined have truth-values they have the same truth-value. On this understanding of the biconditional connective, it does not follow from the Tarski equivalence that if '*S* is true' is false that 'The king of France is wise' is false. What follows from the premise that '*S* is true' is false, on the assumption of the Tarski equivalence, is that either 'The king of France is wise' is false or truth-valueless. It is the latter alternative which Strawson holds to be correct, but this contention does not require him to reject the Tarski equivalences.

8. I have suggested above that an argument against the Tarski equivalences violates Strawson's account of the connectives. Let us call this account the 'conditional' account. The account with which it contrasts, the standard treatment of the connectives, we will call the 'categorical account'. Now I think that it can be shown that Strawson's arguments sometimes rest upon a slide between these two accounts of the connectives and of logical relations. In discussing the relation of presupposition which holds between *S* and *S'*, Strawson observes in *Introduction to Logical Theory* that the assertion of *S* together with the assertion of the negation of *S'* results in a kind of absurdity to be distinguished from the kind of absurdity resulting from the assertion of a statement together with the assertion of the negation of a statement entailed by that statement.[1] In this latter case we have a 'straightforward contradiction'. But since the relation between *S* and *S'*, on Strawson's view, is not that of entailment, he holds that the assertion of '*S* and ~*S'*' is not a 'straightforward contradiction'.

In order to evaluate this reasoning we must know what account to give of the notion of contradiction, for there are two accounts available, the conditional one and the categorical one. Since Strawson asserts that '*S* & ~*S'*' is not a 'straightforward contradiction', he must have the categorical account of that notion in mind, for on the conditional account, '*S* & ~*S'*' is, as

[1] *Introduction to Logical Theory*, p. 175.

we have shown, a contradiction. On the categorical account of contradiction, to say that '$S$ & $\sim S$'' is a contradiction is to say that it is necessarily false. But Strawson hesitates to say that '$S$ & $\sim S$'' is necessarily false because, I suppose, he hesitates to say that the conjunction of a contingently true statement with a contingently truth-valueless one is necessarily false, rather than truth-valueless. But if this is Strawson's reasoning he is sliding between the conditional and the categorical accounts of contradiction. On the conditional account there is no problem. If $S$ is truth-valueless '$S$ & $\sim S$'' is a contradiction. The categorical account, however, applies to propositions and not to statements. At any rate, it applies only to objects which have truth-values. So once again there is no problem. On the categorical account '$S$ & $\sim S$'' does not have a truth-value. It is like the expression $\dfrac{x}{y}$ for $y = $ o. For $y = $ o, $\dfrac{x}{y}$ has no value. So once again, there is no problem.

9. It should be observed that Strawson must abide by the conditional account of logical relations, for classical and modern logic apply to objects (call them 'propositions') which are either true or false. If we introduce an object which is neither of these we can avoid abandoning this logic only by shifting away from the categorical account of these relations. The effect of introducing the conditional account is to enable Strawson both to have his truth-valueless statements and to retain the classical logic rather than to shift to a many-valued system.

Strawson misunderstands what he has done when he claims to have shown that there is a mistake in Russell's theory. What Strawson has really done is to show us how to retain Russell's theory of descriptions, while countenancing truth-valueless objects as values of the variables of logic. Strawson thinks it possible to derive a general moral from his observations concerning the deficiencies of Russell's Theory of Descriptions. 'The general moral of all this is that communication is much less a matter of explicit or disguised assertion than logicians used to suppose.' There is a particular application of this general moral to the case under consideration, the case of making a unique reference. Expressions of the kind we have been studying can be used to make unique references. It is part of the significance of these expressions that they can be so used. But, 'It is no part of their significance to assert that they are being so used or that the conditions of their being so used are fulfilled.' Russell, according to Strawson, arrives at his Theory of Descriptions by confusing a necessary condition for something to be referred to in the use of a uniquely referring expression, with part of what is asserted when such an expression is used as subject of a subject–predicate sentence in the making of a statement. Another way of putting Strawson's point here is to say that Russell, according to Strawson, confuses what is entailed by a statement with what is presupposed by that statement.

In expounding his Theory of Descriptions, Russell never says that part of what one is saying when one says that $S$ is that $S'$. What he says is that the proper *analysis* of $S$ is given by an existentially generalized conjunction. From this conjunction it *follows* that $S'$. So in holding that Russell is committed to the view that in saying $S$ one is also saying (in part) $S'$, Strawson is himself committed to the view that if an $S_1$ is analysed into an $S_2$ and if $S_2$ entails $S_3$ that part of what one is saying in saying $S_1$ is $S_3$. But he gives us no reason to accept *this* assumption. As far as the logic of the situation is concerned, it seems to me that Russell might retort as follows, 'Strawson says that in saying $S$ one presupposes $S'$. But this implies that part of what one is saying in saying $S$ is $S'$.' Strawson would answer correctly, 'No, $S'$ is not part of what one is saying, it is what one is presupposing.' What one is presupposing is contrasted with (not part of) what one is saying. But Russell then could answer, equally correctly, it seems to me, 'No, $S'$ is not part of what one is saying in saying $S$, it is what one entails in saying $S$.' Just as what one presupposes is opposed to what one says, not part of it, so what one implies is opposed to what one says, not part of it.

I think, however, that there is something to Strawson's contention. If a statement entails another, and if the entailment is one which is not at all difficult to grasp, then when someone has said the first statement it would be correct to say that the speaker had (in a certain sense of the verb 'to say') 'said' the statement it entailed. But put in this way (in this sense of 'to say') Strawson's point about what is explicit in communication cannot be made for this is not an explicit sense of 'to say', it is, one might say, an implicit sense. If $p$ entails $q$, and the entailment is obvious and

97

easily grasped, we may say that in saying that $p$ we implicitly say that $q$. But in this sense of the verb, if $p$ presupposes $q$, and the presupposition is obvious and easily grasped, we may with equal correctness say that in saying $p$ we implicitly say that $q$.

10. Strawson's criticisms of Russell's theory may be summarized in two principal contentions. (1) Russell wrongly asserts a relation of entailment to hold between statements of the kind exemplified by 'The present king of France is wise' ($S$) and statements of the kind exemplified by 'One, and only one, person is at present king of France' ($S'$). (2) Russell wrongly asserts that part of what one is saying when one makes a statement of the first kind is a statement of the second kind. Strawson accounts for both of the mistakes which he attributes to Russell in terms of his concept of presupposition. The first of Russell's errors, according to Strawson, is due to his failure to see that it is the relation of presupposition and not that of entailment which holds between statements of the kind $S$ and statements of the kind $S'$. And Russell's second mistake is a consequence of the first. Had Russell seen that statements of the kind $S$ presuppose statements of the kind $S'$, then, according to Strawson, he would not have held the second of his mistaken views.

Against Strawson, I have argued that he is confused in each of his criticisms of Russell. Concerning the first criticism, I have argued that on the account of logical entailment and the logical connectives which he offers (the 'conditional' account) there is not only no contradiction involved in maintaining that statements of the kind $S$ *both* presuppose and entail statements of the kind $S'$ but also that, on this account, the relation of entailment is contained within the relation of presupposition, i.e., that if one statement presupposes another statement it also entails it. Further, Strawson's arguments go nowhere towards showing that $S$ does not entail $S'$ on the standard ('categorical') account of entailment which does not even make sense for truth-valueless objects.

It does not seem to have been generally recognized that Strawson is indeed committed to the existence of truth-valueless statements. This commitment is established by the following argument. By the definition of presupposition cited above from *Introduction to Logical Theory*, $S$ is said to presuppose $S'$ if, and only if, a necessary condition for $S$ having a truth-value is that $S'$ be true.

Since the statement presupposed ($S'$) is false, it follows by this definition that $S$ is neither true nor false.

The substantial point of difference between Strawson and Russell is to be found here. When one utters a sentence such as 'The king of France is wise' is one saying something which must be either true or false as Russell contends, or may one be saying something which is neither true nor false as Strawson contends? I side with Strawson and against Russell on this question. This difference is misconceived as an issue as to whether a relation of entailment obtains. It is better viewed as a disagreement as to whether in our everyday discourse we speak in statements or in propositions. If, as I believe, Strawson is right on this question, what is required is a new account of the connectives of logic and of logical relations such as entailment, which will enable us to talk sensibly about the logic of statements (in Strawson's sense). Strawson has attempted to provide such an account. But it does not follow from any of this that there is a mistake in Russell's analysis of the proposition 'The present king of France is wise'.

# VII

# PURE REFERENCE

1. Quine, Frege, and Russell approach problems connected with *oratio obliqua* constructions determined to defend Leibniz's Law, the principle of substitutivity, sometimes referred to as 'the indiscernibility of identicals'. The principle states that, 'Given a true statement of identity, one of its two terms may be substituted for the other in any true statement and the result will be true.'[1] The 'law', however, it seems, is just false, for it is possible that Smith knows that Venus is the morning star and yet does not know that Venus is the evening star, though, 'The morning star is the evening star' is a 'true statement of identity'. Again, from

(1) Cicero is Tully,

and

(2) 'Cicero' is spelled with six letters.

it does not follow that

(3) 'Tully' is spelled with six letters.

Not only is it possible to produce counter-examples to Leibniz's Law, it can be shown that no two terms obey it. Let $t$ and $t'$ be different terms and consider any true statement of the form

(4) Jones explicitly denied that $t = t'$.

Surely one cannot substitute $t$ for $t'$ in (4) in order validly to obtain

(5) Jones explicitly denied that $t = t$.

---

[1] *From a Logical Point of View*, by W. V. Quine, Harvard, 1953, p. 139. For me, the principle of substitutivity and the indiscernibility of identicals are different principles. Cf. Chapter V, section 10.

No statement of the form (5) follows from the corresponding statement of the form (4), even though $t = t'$ be true. If one insists that the principle of substitutivity is analytic and explicative of the concept of identity one is faced with the peculiar consequence that only trivial statements of the form $t = t$ are true statements of identity. A true statement of identity can never be informative.

It will be instructive to go into Quine's 'way out', for his 'solution' does illuminate the nature of our problem. According to Quine, positions in sentences for which the principle of substitutivity is not a valid mode of inference are 'referentially opaque' ones. They are positions such that expressions occupying them do not succeed in referring to anything, although the very same expressions will refer in other, referentially open, positions. Thus, in the statement 'Smith knows that Venus is the morning star' the two positions flanking 'is' are referentially opaque. Similarly, the position between the quotation marks in (2) is referentially opaque. Thus failure of substitutivity in these cases does not provide exceptions to Leibniz's Law, but only cases of referential opacity.

'Very well,' an objector might argue, 'what Quine has really shown is not that Leibniz's Law has no exceptions. What he has done is to have given a characterization of the exceptions. He says that they involve substitution into referentially opaque positions. If he insists, nevertheless, that the principle of substitutivity admits of no exceptions he must be defending it not as it is formulated above, but in another version which goes as follows: "Given a true statement of identity, one of its two terms may be substituted for the other at any referentially open position in a true statement, *salva veritate*." '

The well-known examples involving so-called verbs of propositional attitude will not provide counter-examples to *this* principle. Substitution positions within clauses governed by these verbs are not referentially open. For what is the criterion of the referential opacity of a position? It is just that the principle of substitutivity in its first (unamended) form fails to be a valid mode of inference with respect to that position. The principle in its revised form is just the principle in its original form with the addition of a clause, which in effect tells us that counter-examples do not count. Clearly there are no counter-examples to *this* principle.

It should be clear that what is under discussion is what Quine calls 'the principle of the indiscernibility of identicals' and not its trivial converse, the identity of indiscernibles. This latter principle says that if two terms $t$ and $t'$ are interchangeable in every true statement, *salva veritate*, then $t = t'$ is a true statement. The following argument quickly establishes that this is so. If $t$ and $t'$ are interchangeable in every true statement, *salva veritate*, they are interchangeable in the true statement $t = t$. Therefore, replacing the right-hand $t$ by $t'$ we get $t = t'$, *salva veritate*.

2. Let us accept, for the present, the ideas of pure reference and impure reference as sufficiently clear for our purposes. Let us suppose that is, that in virtue of our understanding of our language we possess the ability to distinguish cases in which terms perform their purely referential function from cases in which they fail to do so. In 'Scott is the author of *Waverley*', 'Scott' performs its function of referring simply to its bearer, Scott. In 'George IV wished to know whether Scott was the author of *Waverley*', 'the author of *Waverley*' does not have pure reference to Scott. In terms of the semantical relation of pure reference we can account for the failures of substitutivity already noted. But we must not in turn explain pure reference by appeal solely to the principle of substitutivity. For then the claim that the principle is correct only for terms in their purely referential occurrences reduces, as we have seen, to the claim that the principle is correct except when it is not correct.

Let us further grant, for the present (we shall want to question this shortly), that failure of substitutivity reveals merely that a term is not performing its purely referential function. Is it the case that if substitutivity for a term does not fail that term *is* performing its purely referential function? No. Consider the statement

(6) 'Cicero' is a designation for Cicero.

Substitution on the basis of (1) produces

(7) 'Tully' is a designation for Cicero,

which is true, as is (6). *Any* substitution for 'Cicero' in its first occurrence in (6) on the basis of a true statement of identity containing it as one of its terms will go through *salva veritate*. Yet

'Cicero' does not have pure reference in that occurrence. Another example in aid of the same conclusion is

(8) 'Cicero' $\neq$ with Cicero.

'Cicero' may be replaced in its first occurrence in the true statement (8) by any term at all *salva veritate*. Yet 'Cicero' paradigmatically lacks pure reference in this occurrence.

In one text, Quine defines a 'referentially opaque' context as follows. 'We may speak of a context as *referentially opaque* when by putting a statement $\phi$ into that context, we can cause a purely referential occurrence in $\phi$ to be not purely referential in the whole context.'[1] Thus in

(9) Cicero is a designation for Cicero,

the name 'Cicero' is purely designative in both of its occurrences. But the result of inserting (9) into the context of quotation (or better, the result of inserting the context of quotation into *it*) is the statement (6), in which the first occurrence of 'Cicero' is no longer purely designative. 'Quotation,' says Quine, 'is the referentially opaque context *par excellance*.'[2]

Failure of substitutivity, then, is not a necessary condition for the non-purely referential occurrence of a term. Here are two further (non-quotational) examples.

(10) Charles de Gaulle is not the king of France.

This statement is straightforwardly true. Replacement of 'the king of France' in (10) on the basis of the true identity,

(11) The king of France = the most frequently cited example of a non-existent object,

goes through *salva veritate*. So would the replacement of this term by any other term joining it in a true identity statement go through *salva veritate*. But the term 'the king of France' in (10) cannot for Quine be said to have pure reference to its object, for notoriously, 'its object' does not exist.

We reach another (non-quotational) example of impure reference without failure of substitutivity by consideration of the true statement '$N(9 > 7)$'.[3] Here '9' has impure reference and

---

[1] W. V. Quine. 'Three Grades of Modal Involvement' in *The Ways of Paradox*, Random House, New York, 1966, p. 158.
[2] *Ibid.*, p. 159.
[3] '$N$' is short for 'It is logically necessary that'.

substitutivity fails, for though '9 = the number of the planets' is true, replacement of the right-hand term of this identity for the left-hand term turns our truth into the false statement '$N$ (the number of the planets $> 7$)'. But if '9' lacks pure reference in '$N(9 > 7)$', surely it must also in '$N(9 \not> 7)$'. This latter is false and remains false under every replacement '9' by any other designation for 9. But '$\sim N(9 \not> 7)$' is true under the same conditions. So here we have a case of impure reference unaccompanied by failure of substitutivity.

3. Is failure of substitutivity a sufficient condition for the non-purely referential occurrence of a term? No. Suppose Lyndon B. Johnson to be the chairman of the Harvard Philosophy Department. Then,

(12) The person who holds the office of president of the United States = the person who holds the office of chairman of the Harvard Philosophy Department.

is a true statement of identity. It is also true that

(13) The person who holds the office of president of the United States was administered the oath of the latter office by the Chief Justice of the Supreme Court.

Surely, if there is such a thing as a relation of pure reference at all, the term 'the person who holds the office of president of the United States' stands in (13) in that relation to Lyndon B. Johnson. But replacement of that term on the basis of (12) yields the false statement

(14) The person who holds the office of chairman of the Harvard Philosophy Department was administered the oath of the latter office by the Chief Justice of the Supreme Court.

Here we have failure of substitutivity together with pure reference. Failure of substitutivity is therefore neither a necessary nor a sufficient condition for non-pure reference. What, then, of the principle of substitutivity? Unless we can find some characteristic common to all cases of its failure, we are left defending a principle as correct in all cases except where it fails.

There are, it seems, at least two alternatives available to us. *Alternative I.* We can try to find another characteristic common to all cases of failure of substitutivity, perhaps a disjunctive one, e.g., every case of failure involves either (1) non-purely referential occurrence of a term or (2) a demonstrative expression (e.g., 'the latter office'). We can now claim to have, in terms of this disjunctive characteristic, a *necessary condition* of failure of substitutivity, though certainly not a sufficient condition. *Alternative II*. Since we cannot find a condition which is both necessary and sufficient for failure of substitutivity, we can frankly admit that we are in a circle. We can that is, *define* referential opacity (nonextensionality) in terms of failure of substitutivity. It is then, of course, true that the principle of substitutivity holds only for referentially open positions. This is, in fact, what Carnap does.[1] It is also what Frege does, I believe. But since Frege's discussion of these matters is highly informal, it is hard to be sure about his position in this regard. Quine slides between Alternative I and Alternative II. He seems to be taking Alternative II, for example, when in the essay 'Reference and Modality', he says that failure of substitutivity is his 'criterion' of referential occurrence.[2]

*Difficulties with Alternative I.* We began by adopting an uncritical attitude towards the ideas of pure and impure reference. We began by assuming that the distinction between pure and impure reference was something that we could recognize without appeal to consideration of failure of substitutivity. It is now time to question that assumption. It is my view that the distinction is a logical mirage. What Quine does is to introduce his distinction with the aid of examples. 'Crassus heard Tully denounce Catiline', for example, exhibits three terms having pure reference to their objects. Quotation exhibits impure reference paradigmatically. Now with our logical eyes fixed upon the paradigm cases we turn to statements involving propositional attitudes and the logical modalities. We are supposed to see the same phenomenon of impure reference in these cases that we previously saw provided by the context of quotation. What we in fact see, if we see anything at all, is a mere negative after image, produced by staring overly long at the context of quotation.

What is the similarity between cases of quotation, on the one hand, and cases of the propositional attitudes and logical modalities, on the other, supposed to consist in? What is the similarity

---

[1] *Meaning and Necessity*, Chicago, 1956, pp. 47–8. On this alternative, the subject position in (13) is by definition referentially opaque.
[2] *From a Logical Point of View*, p. 140.

between ' "9" is a numeral' and '$N(9 > 7)$' with respect to the semantics of '9'? In the first statement nothing is said about a number at all. There is surely a difference here, for if '9' refers impurely to 9 in the second statement, it does not refer to 9 at all in the first. Then what is the difference between the relation which '9' bears to 9 in '$N(9 > 7)$' and the relation which it bears to that number in '$9 > 7$'? Why is this not pure reference again? We cannot appeal to failure of substitutivity as establishing the impurity in '$N(9 > 7)$', for then Alternative I collapses into Alternative II.

4. *Difficulties with Alternative II.* According to this alternative, referential opacity (impure reference) is defined in terms of failure of substitutivity. Consider this argument due to Kalish and Montague.

> Alcibiades is the most notorious Athenian traitor. Everyone believes that Alcibiades is honest. Therefore, everyone believes that the most notorious Athenian traitor is honest.[1]

Surely this argument is invalid, for it is *possible* for the premises to be true and the conclusion false. Note, however, that in fact, the second premise of the argument is false. We cannot explain the fallacy by claiming that the conclusion arises from the premises via an illegitimate substitution into a referentially opaque (or non-extensional) context, for if failure of substitutivity is the criterion of referential opacity (as it is, according to Alternative II), there is no reason to regard the second premise as referentially opaque. 'Everyone believes that Alcibiades is honest' is false. This statement remains false under every substitution of alternative names or designations for 'Alcibiades'; there is no designation for Alcibiades under which *everyone* believes that he is honest. (Consider the six-month-old infant. It does not believe that Alcibiades, under any designation, is honest.) Therefore, by the criterion of substitutivity, 'Everyone believes that Alcibiades is honest' is referentially transparent.

Kalish and Montague take the heroic seeming course of declaring the argument under consideration to be a valid one. They say, 'It is not to be expected that all unsatisfactory examples are precluded by the requirement of extensionality. Indeed, there are

[1] *Logic*, by Kalish and Montague, Harcourt, Brace, New York, 1964, p. 229.

English arguments that completely fulfil the requirements for validity . . . but that on intuitive grounds would tend to be regarded as invalid.' They say further, by way of apology (it seems), 'Indeed, it is not to be expected that a completely precise analysis of validity for a natural language, faithfully reflecting all intuitions that have accrued during the historical development of the language, could be either simple, elegant, or of major philosophical interest.'[1] The definition of extensionality given by Kalish and Montague is essentially the same as that employed by Carnap, Frege, and Quine. Their definition is this: 'An English *sentence* $\phi$ is said to be extensional if, whenever a name occurring in it is replaced in one or more of its occurrences by another name designating the same object, the resulting sentence has the same truth value as $\phi$, that is, is true or false according as $\phi$ is true or false.'[2]

There is one way of avoiding the difficulty presented by the Alcibiades example. We can change the definition of extensionality so that a sentence is said to be extensional (referentially transparent), not if a change of truth value does not occur but only if a change of truth value cannot (as a matter of logic) occur when one name is replaced by another name for the same thing in that sentence. According to this definition, the statement 'Everyone believes that Alcibiades is honest' is non-extensional (referentially opaque). We have only to imagine a possible world in which humans are less suspicious of their fellow men, and in which six-month-old babies are fully informed about the world in which they live. In this world 'Everyone believes that Alcibiades is honest' is true, not false. The falsity of the conclusion 'Everyone believes that the most notorious Athenian traitor is honest', now is seen simply as establishing the referential opacity of the second premise. We can now safely declare the whole argument invalid in accordance with our intuitions.

There is, however, the following difficulty in thus proceeding. Our definition of referential opacity employs the concept of logical possibility. But logical possibility is a notion which we wish to characterize as referentially opaque. We have therefore entered a vicious circle. Further, Quine claims not to be able to make sense of the logical modalities in general and therefore of

---

[1] *Logic*, by Kalish and Montague, Harcourt, Brace, New York, 1964, p. 230.
[2] *Ibid.*, p. 215.

logical possibility. He cannot accept our account of opacity in terms of possibility without committing himself to the unintelligibility of the first notion.[1] The main difficulty with this alternative, however, is that it keeps us within the circle described in section 1.

5. Consider the following argument presented by Quine, 'Think of $p$ as short for some statement, and think of $F(p)$ as short for some containing true statement, such that the context represented by $F$ is not referentially opaque. Suppose further that the context represented by $F$ is such that logical equivalents are interchangeable, within it, *salva veritate*. . . . What I shall show is that the occurrence of $p$ in $F(p)$ is then truth-functional. I.e., think of $q$ as short for some statement having the same truth value as $p$; I shall show that $F(q)$ is, like $F(p)$, true.'[2] In other words, what this argument is supposed to establish concerning $F$ is that if it is not referentially opaque, and admits interchange of logically equivalent statements, *salva veritate*, it is truth-functional. Or again, if we suppose an $F$ such that it admits interchange of logically equivalent statements it follows that $F$ is either truth-functional or referentially opaque. Still another way: We cannot have interchangeability of logical equivalents and depart from the policy of extensionality (the policy of admitting only truth-functional modes of statement composition) without accepting referential opacity. This, on Quine's view, is a reason for not departing from the policy of extensionality.

Here is the argument which establishes this conclusion. What $p$ represents is a statement, either true or false. Suppose $p$ is true. Then the conjunction, $x = \Lambda \ \& \ p$ is true of one, and only one, object $x$, viz., $\Lambda$; if $p$ is false the same conjunction is true of nothing ($\Lambda$ is a name for the null class). The class $\hat{X}(X = \Lambda \ \& \ p)$, therefore, is $\iota\Lambda$ or $\Lambda$ (where $\iota\Lambda$ is the class whose only member is $\Lambda$) according as $p$ is true or false. The equation

$$(15) \quad \hat{X}(X = \Lambda \ \& \ p) = \iota\Lambda$$

---

[1] Under the proposed account of extensionality, '(Everyone believes that Alcibiades is honest) or $(9 > 7)$' is extensional, since the right disjunct is a necessary truth. This yields the surprising result that in this statement 'Alcibiades' has pure reference to its object, though it has impure reference to the same object in 'Everyone believes that Alcibiades is honest'. This result would surely be unacceptable to Quine.
[2] *Ways of Paradox*, p. 161.

is logically equivalent, by the above considerations, to $p$. Since $F(p)$ is true, and logically equivalent statements are interchangeable within it, it follows that

$$(16)\ F[\hat{X}(X = \varLambda\ \&\ p) = \iota\varLambda]$$

is true. Since $p$ and $q$ have the same truth value, the classes $\hat{X}(X = \varLambda\ \&\ p)$ and $\hat{X}(X = \varLambda\ \&\ q)$ are both either $\iota\varLambda$ or $\varLambda$. Therefore,

$$(17)\ \hat{X}(X = \varLambda\ \&\ p) = \hat{X}(X = \varLambda\ \&\ q).$$

Since the context represented by $F$ is not referentially opaque, the occurrence of $\hat{X}(X = \varLambda\ \&\ p)$ in (16) is purely referential. So by (17) and the principle of substitutivity we conclude

$$(18)\ F[\hat{X}(X = \varLambda\ \&\ q) = \iota\varLambda].$$

Now since $\hat{X}(X = \varLambda\ \&\ q) = \iota\varLambda$ is logically equivalent to $q$ we conclude that $F(q)$, Q.E.D.

Thus, Quine's argument. If what has earlier been said about pure reference is correct, what is the significance of this result? The argument is supposed to show that departure from the policy of extensionality, for a certain class of cases, entails acceptance of referentially opaque constructions. For Quine, this argument carries weight as an argument for extensionalism, because he sees referentially opaque contexts on the model of quotational ones in which singular terms do not occur at all, in any logically relevant way. From Quine's point of view, acceptance of referentially opaque contexts involves us in a mistake in logical analysis. The mistake, in essence, consists in taking singular terms to occur in contexts in which, from a logical point of view, they are not present in any relevant sense. Thus Quine's 'flight from intentions'. Now all of this would make sense in terms of a clear distinction between pure and impure reference. But if what has been said is correct the only clear sense that is attached to the notion of impure reference is failure of substitutivity. If all that is clearly meant by saying that a term has impure reference is that substitutivity fails for that term in some position one can turn Quine's argument against the conclusion he seeks to establish. For then, does not the argument show that the policy of extensionality is a reasonable one only from the vantage point of an overly simple view of the functioning of singular terms?

Quine's argument would support his conclusion only if he had succeeded in showing that the revisions of the logic of singular terms which acceptance of referentially opaque contexts impose on us are really not necessary. But it seems more reasonable to view the policy of extensionality as arising from a determined adherence to the principle of substitutivity in the face of well-known counter-examples. Modification or abandonment of this principle is certainly part of what is involved in the modification of the logic of singular terms which Quine's argument shows to be entailed by deviation from the extensional point of view (at least for the restricted class of cases which Quine's argument concerns).

6. Reference and quantification are, for Quine, just as intimately associated as are reference and substitutivity. Quine holds that singular terms are all eliminable by paraphrase. Then does referential opacity disappear with singular terms? A referentially opaque context is just one in which singular terms fail to perform their purely referential function. According to Quine, referential opacity does not disappear with singular terms. It lingers on to inhibit the free use of quantifiers. 'Ultimately,' he says, 'the objects referred to in a theory are to be accounted not as the things named by the singular terms, but as the values of the variables of quantification. So if referential opacity is an in-firmity worth worrying about, it must show symptoms in con-nection with quantification as well as in connection with singular terms.' [1]

Referential opacity, on Quine's view, does display the expected symptoms in connection with quantification. The connection is direct and startling. Quantification into referentially opaque con-texts produces *nonsense*. The connection between pure reference and quantification is displayed in the operation called 'existential generalization'. Existential generalization is justified by the truism that whatever is true of the object named by some singular term is true of something. So, for example, from 'Socrates is the teacher of Plato', we infer by existential generalization, '$(\exists x)$ ($x$ is the teacher of Plato)'. But from

(19) There is no such thing as Pegasus,

[1] *From a Logical Point of View*, pp. 144-5.

it does not follow that

(20) $(\exists x)$ (there is no such thing as $x$).

Failure of existential generalization from (19) to (20) is a consequence of the fact that 'Pegasus' in (19) does not have pure reference to its object. Quine holds that this inference is equally unwarranted for terms in all of their non-purely referential occurrences. Such quantifications are one and all nonsense, and Quine sees in these abortive quantifications an alternative criterion of referential opacity. Can we then give as an explanation for apparent failures of substitutivity that they all arise from misapplication of the principle of substitutivity to terms in non-purely referential occurrences; understanding this latter to be what a term has in a context in which attempted existential generalization aborts into nonsense?

This approach certainly has its attractions, for if we take it we can avoid the most severe objection to Alternative II. We can adhere to the principle of substitutivity and dismiss the apparent counter-examples as arising through misapplication to terms not performing their purely referential task, and we can give a meaning to this latter notion without appealing to the test of failure of substitutivity itself; we can appeal to failure of quantification instead. The approach, however, will not do. The reason is that the quantifications which Quine wishes to prohibit are certainly not nonsense. Consider the statement

(21) Jones believes that somebody stole the jewels.

This statement can be understood in two quite different ways. It can be understood as meaning that Jones believes the jewels were stolen by somebody or other. Or the statement can be understood as meaning that there is some one definite person whom Jones believes to have stolen the jewels. That is (21) can be understood either as

(22) Jones believes $(\exists x)$ ($x$ stole the jewels)

or as

(23) $(\exists x)$ (Jones believes $x$ stole the jewels).

There are, of course, any number of such examples. Consider

(24) Jones wants a wife.

This can mean either that Jones wishes to terminate his state of bachelorhood. Thus

(25) Jones wants that $(\exists x)$ ($x$ becomes the wife of Jones).

On the other hand, (24) *can* be understood to mean that Jones covets somebody else's wife, thus

(26) $(\exists x)\{(x$ is a wife$)$ & $($Jones wants $x)\}$.

The point of the examples is that since (21) and (24) can be understood as (23) and (26) respectively, and since these statements are perfectly intelligible thus understood, *it must be false that quantification into referentially opaque contexts always produces nonsense.*

Any view, such as Quine's, which makes it impossible for quantifiers to bind variables within the scope of verbs of propositional attitude is inadequate as an account of the interaction between singular terms and quantification. Quine does not merely declare these quantifications to be nonsense, however, he gives an argument which purports to prove that they are. The argument is this. Consider the statement

(27) $(\exists x)$ (George IV wishes to know if $x$ is the author of *Waverley*).

Who is this person concerning whom George IV entertained his curiosity? Presumably it is Scott, i.e., the author of *Waverley*. But though it is true that

(28) George IV wishes to know if Scott is the author of *Waverley*.

it is also true that

(29) George IV does not wish to know if the author of *Waverley* is the author of *Waverley*.

The criticism of (27) comes to this. Its acceptance commits us to the acceptance of unacceptable consequences. An existential generalization entails the existence of at least one object within the range of values of the quantifier which satisfies the open sentence containing the variable bound by that quantifier. With (27), the required individual seems forthcoming, but the attempt to state who he is drives us into the apparent contradiction involved in asserting both (28) and (29).

No one, of course, holds that (27) is a statement of English. What I maintain is that there is a perfectly good statement of English which involves the binding of a variable within the scope of an existential quantifier. This is the statement (21) understood as saying that Jones believes that some specific person (unnamed) stole the jewels. If this is not a case in which such binding of a variable occurs, I cannot imagine what would be.

I think that the correct conclusion to be drawn here is quite different from the one Quine draws. (27), (28), and (29) are indeed true. Certainly there is something paradoxical about the joint assertion of the latter two in view of the identity of Scott and the author of *Waverley*. But the joint assertion of the following two statements is equally paradoxical in view of that identity:

(30) Scott is tall.

and

(31) The author of *Waverley* is not tall.

Is it possible for (30) and (31) both to be true? Suppose that we are comparing Scott, i.e., the author of *Waverley*, to two different standards: a short person and a tall person. Then both (30) and (31), properly understood, are true. Scott, i.e., the author of *Waverley*, is tall in comparison with one person and not tall in comparison with another. The air of paradox in the joint assertion of (30) and (31) is removed once it is realized that they contain suppressed reference to different standards of comparison. Once the suppressed term is referred to explicitly, the air of paradox disappears.

I wish to suggest that being identical with something or other under the scope of a verb of propositional attitude is logically a more than dyadic relation. The air of paradox occasioned by the joint assertion of (28) and (29), I suggest, results from failure to make explicit the nature of this relation and the possibly suppressed terms it involves. A first attempt (surely inadequate) towards removing the paradox along these lines might analyse (28) and (29) respectively as

(32) George IV wishes to know if Scott, under the designation 'Scott', is the author of *Waverley*,

and

(33) George IV does not wish to know if Scott, under the designation 'the author of *Waverley*', is the author of *Waverley*.

6. Why does Liebniz's Law, the principle of substitutivity, fail? We have examined one attempt to provide an answer in terms of the distinction between purely and impurely referential occurrences of terms. We have found that account unsatisfactory. Can another, more satisfactory, one be given? I shall try now to provide one. It is not my aim to explain all failures of substitutivity but only those which arise in connection with the *oratio obliqua* mode of speech and the employment of verbs of propositional attitude, 'believes', 'hopes', 'wishes', 'knows', 'expects', etc. For convenience, I shall refer to all of these cases as *oratio obliqua* cases, even when strictly verbs of saying do not occur.

Suppose that I am a receptionist for the President of the United States. Suppose, further, that I am a friend of the family and that I regularly use their first names in addressing the President and his wife. Suppose a minor official approaches me and asks, 'Will the President be able to see me sometime before 11.00 today?' I call the White House and the President's wife answers. I say, 'There is an official here who wishes to know if Lyndon can see him before 11.00.' Is what I said false? Certainly not. Yet my words deviate from those actually used by the official. He said, 'Will the President be able to see me before 11.00?' When, in *oratio obliqua*, I report the content of the official's desire, I use the name 'Lyndon' where he used the term 'the President'. In *oratio obliqua* I am not responsible for reproducing the very words in which a person expresses his propositional attitude. That, one might say, is the whole reason for the existence of this mode of speech. That is what distinguishes it from the *oratio recta* mode. Of the extreme utility of the *oratio obliqua* form there cannot be any doubt. Imagine the burden which we would take upon ourselves in reporting what others say or want to know if in doing so we were not allowed to deviate from the very words they used in saying what they said or expressing what they want or know.

What the indirect forms allow us to do is to convey the content without reproducing the words. How far are we allowed to stray from the actual words spoken? There is, of course, no fixed line over which one must not pass without falling into falsity. The governing rule here is that *one must not mislead one's audience.* Whether or not one's words are misleading or false depends upon complex features of the setting in which one speaks, including principally what one knows or believes that one's audience knows or believes. It is absurd to suggest that in reporting another's words in indirect discourse *any* deviation renders my account false. For the conventions governing the use of this mode of speech are not such that my audience will take me *not* to be deviating from the actual words I am reporting in *oratio obliqua* construction. In general, the dichotomy, true or false, seems less in place here than the dichotomies, fair/unfair or accurate/inaccurate. What one wants is a fair or accurate account of what someone said or knows or wants. The reporter's obligation is not to mislead in his deviations; it is *not* not to deviate.

We can now see why a form of speech exists in which the kind of 'failure' of substitutivity so much attended to by Frege, Carnap, Quine, and others is possible. To eliminate forms in which such 'failure' can occur is to eliminate indirect discourse. And this, in a sense, is an explanation as to why the principle of substitutivity fails. Because, in natural languages, we have (and cannot dispense with) this mode of speech. This situation is not immediately open to the logician's view because of his tendency to talk of 'statements' or 'propositions' in abstraction from actual speech situations which involve, along with these statements, both speakers and audiences. He then notes that, e.g., though it is true that Oedipus wanted to marry Jocasta and that Jocasta was the mother of Oedipus, it is not true that Oedipus wanted to marry his mother. But note that if one is speaking to an audience that knows the story there is no objection at all to saying 'Oedipus wanted to marry his mother'. One may say this last to an audience which knows that Oedipus was unaware of the fact that his mother satisfies the open sentence 'x = Jocasta'. Such an audience will not regard the statement 'Oedipus wanted to marry his mother' as false, as the logicians say it is, much less will they regard it as misleading or an unfair or inaccurate account of what Oedipus wanted. In fact, given the speech situation envisaged, there is nothing at all wrong with saying 'Oedipus wanted to marry his mother'.

# VIII
## REFERENCE AND REFERENTS

1. In discussing the topics of definite descriptions, referring expressions, and proper names, mistakes are made due to a failure to distinguish referring and making a reference, in the ordinary meanings of these terms, from what philosophers call 'denoting' and 'referring'. Of first importance here is the consideration that it is the users of language who refer and make references and not, except in a derivative sense, the expressions which they use in so doing. Ryle, for example, says, 'A descriptive phrase is not a proper name, and the way in which the subject of attributes which it denotes is denoted by it is not in that subject's being *called* "the so-and-so", but in its possessing and being *ipso facto* the sole possessor of the idiosyncratic attribute which is what the descriptive phrase signifies.' [1] I do not wish to deny that what Ryle says here is true, in his technical sense of 'denote'. The example is chosen only to bring out how different this sense is from what we ordinarily understand by 'referring'. I might, for example, refer to someone as 'the old man with grey hair'. Still, the phrase 'the old man with grey hair' does not 'signify' an 'idiosyncratic attribute', if what is meant by this is an attribute belonging to just *one* person. It is equally obvious that I might refer to a person as 'the so-and-so', even though that person did not possess the attribute (idiosyncratic or not) 'signified' by that phrase. I might, for example, refer to someone as 'the old man with grey hair', even though that person was not old but prematurely grey. In both cases I would be referring to someone not 'denoted' (in Ryle's sense) by the expression used in so doing. But these *expressions*

[1] 'Systematically Misleading Expressions', reprinted in *Essays on Logic and Language*, ed. by A. Flew, New York, 1951, p. 23.

do not refer to that person, I do. The question 'To whom does the phrase "the so-and-so" refer?' is, in general, an odd question. What might be asked is, e.g., 'Who is the President of the United States?' or 'To whom are you referring?'; not 'To whom does the phrase "the President of the United States" refer?'

The question 'to whom (what) does the phrase "the so-and-so" refer?' is generally odd. It is not always odd. Certainly it sounds odder in some cases than in others. I think one might ask, 'To what does the phrase "the morning star" refer?' Or, pointing to a written text, I might ask, 'To whom is the author referring with the phrase "the most influential man in Lincoln's cabinet"?' But, in speaking about referring, philosophers have written as though one might sensibly ask such questions in an unlimited number of cases. What else could have caused Russell to say in 'On Denoting', 'A phrase may denote ambiguously; e.g., "a man" denotes not many men, but an ambiguous man?'[1]

It is, of course, perfectly true that one can ask, 'To whom does the pronoun "he" refer?', if one is oneself referring to a particular passage in a text, or to something which has just been said. But it does not follow that one can ask this question *apart* from such a context. Clearly, the question 'to whom does "he" refer?' is a senseless question unless such a context is indicated. The same is true of Russell's example, 'a man'. It is senseless to ask 'To whom does "a man" refer?'; or (using Russell's term), 'Whom does "a man" denote?' But even when the context is clearly indicated, this question does not *always* make sense. If, for example, I tell you that I need a wife, you can hardly ask me, 'To whom are you referring?'

Failure clearly to mark these distinctions leads to confusions about uniqueness of reference. Russell says that a definite description, '. . . will only have an application in the event of there being one so-and-so and no more.'[2] But can I not refer to someone as 'the old madman', even though he is not mad and more than one man is? Does my phrase not have 'application' to the one to whom I am referring? Certainly, I was speaking of him. What is usually said here is that uniqueness of reference is secured by making the description more determinate, e.g., by saying, 'the

[1] Logic and Language, p. 41.
[2] *Principia Mathematica*, I, p. 30.

old man who lives next door'. But this attempt to secure uniqueness of reference through increased determination of the 'referring
expression' is otiose, for what secures uniqueness is the user of the
expression and the context in which it is used *together* with the
expression.

We may now notice Ryle's futile attempt to get uniqueness of
reference somehow guaranteed by the words themselves. 'Tommy
Jones is not the same person as the king of England' means, Ryle
says, what is meant by: '(1) Somebody, and—of an unspecified
circle—one person only is called Tommy Jones; (2) Somebody,
and one person only has royal power in England; and (3) No one
both is called Tommy Jones and is king of England.' But surely
when I say, 'Tommy Jones is not king of England' I am not
claiming that exactly one person of any circle is named 'Tommy
Jones'. What is indeed necessary, if I am to make a definite assertion, is not that one person only be named 'Tommy Jones'; but
that I be referring to just one person, however many others there
may be with the same name as his. It is a mistake to think that
the 'referring expression' itself can secure and guarantee this
uniqueness. This is obvious in the case of proper names, for here
we cannot appeal to meaning. 'Tommy Jones' does not have a
meaning, and many people share it. Proper names are usually
(rather) common names.

Ryle's account makes it appear that it is an intrinsic characteristic of certain groups of words that they denote something or
other. They possess this characteristic in virtue of their 'signifying
an idiosyncratic attribute'. Perhaps he is thinking of such an
expression as 'the oldest American university'. It is a matter of
fact that the oldest American university is Harvard. But nothing
prevents one from referring to another school (by mistake, or in
jest) with these words.

Perhaps Ryle has confused referring to something with referring to it correctly as this or that. I might, for example, refer to
L.W. in saying, 'He is the president of the bank.' Still I would
have referred to him incorrectly as the president of the bank,
because he is not the president of the bank, but the vice president.
Some of what Ryle says will be correct if we interpret his comments about denoting as giving an account of what it is to refer
to something *correctly* as such and such. But it is, after all, possible
to refer to something incorrectly as such and such, and that is

still to refer to it. Furthermore, for one to refer correctly to something as 'the such and such' it is not necessary that the thing referred to be the sole possessor of the 'property signified' by the phrase, though it must certainly have that property. Looked at conversely, we can say that it is not necessary that the property 'signified' by a phrase of the form 'the such and such' be 'idio-syncratic' if one is to refer to something correctly as 'the such and such'.

2. The question, 'To whom (what) does the phrase "the so and so" refer?' is generally odd. But it is not always odd. I am arguing that the sense in which expressions (as opposed to speakers) can be said to refer to things is derivative. I mean by this that the question 'To whom (what) does the phrase "the so and so" refer?' means the same as the question with regard to some person, 'To whom (what) is that person referring with the phrase "the so and so"?' Where the question cannot be so rephrased, it cannot be asked at all, e.g., 'To whom does the pronoun "he" refer?', 'To whom does the phrase "the old man" refer?'

Much of the philosophical discussion of this topic has assumed that this was not so. Russell says that a denoting phrase is such 'solely in virtue of its form'. Thus we should be able to ask 'To whom does the phrase "the tallest man in the prison" refer?', for the denoting phrase here is of the same form as 'The Sultan of Swat', and this phrase can be said to refer to someone, viz., Babe Ruth. But the first question cannot be asked. The second question, 'To whom does the phrase "The Sultan of Swat" refer?' does not require a special context and is not the same question as the one which asks with regard to some person 'To whom was he refer-ring with that phrase?' For clearly this last question might receive a different answer than the first. This would occur if the speaker in question had erroneously been referring to Mickey Mantle. So the question 'To whom does "the so and so" refer?' seems not always to be the same question as the one with regard to some person, 'To whom was he referring with the phrase "the so and so"?'

I am claiming that the counter-examples are only apparent and that the general thesis is still true. There is a class of expressions which (using Strawson's happy description) have grown capital letters. Some examples are 'The Sultan of Swat', 'The Morning

Star', 'The City of the Angels'. One can ask, 'To what city does the phrase "The City of the Angels" refer?' The answer is 'Los Angeles'. Such expressions are on their way to becoming names, e.g. 'The Beast of Belsen'. They are what a thing or person is called often and repeatedly, and that is why one can ask to what they refer. Philosophers were perhaps concentrating on such examples as these when they said or implied that the question 'To whom (what) does "the so and so" refer?' can always be asked. But it cannot.

Perhaps another source of this mistake derives from a confusion between meaning and referring. One can ask both 'What does this phrase mean?' and 'Whom do you mean?' Also 'I referred to so and so' and 'I meant so and so' seem very close indeed. But these verbs are radically different, as can be seen from the following considerations. One can ask, 'Why did you refer to him?', but not, 'Why did you mean him?' One can say, 'Don't refer to him!', but not 'Don't mean him!' 'How often did you refer to him?' is a sensible question, but 'How often did you mean him?' is not. One can ask, 'Why do you refer to him as the such and such?', but not 'Why do you mean him as the such and such?' I can ask why you refer to him at all; but not why you mean him at all. The verb 'to mean' has non-continuous present tense forms, e.g., 'I mean you'; but it lacks the present progressive tense form, 'I am meaning you'. The verb 'to refer' has a present progressive form, 'I am referring to you', as well as a non-continuous present form, 'I refer to Adlai Stevenson'.

What these grammatical considerations show is that referring to someone is an action; meaning someone is not an action. As an action it can be right or wrong for one to perform. Thus it can be wrong of you to refer to someone; but not wrong of you to mean someone. It can be important or necessary that you refer to someone, but not important or necessary that you mean someone. One can intend to refer to someone, but not intend to mean him.

3. In discussions of statements such as 'Edward VII is the king of England' it is sometimes said that in making them one is referring to the same person twice. Frege says that the person is referred to in different ways each time. This way of looking at them leads to their interpretation as identities. But consider the

following conversation to see how odd it is to talk of referring twice to the same person in such contexts:

A: He is the king of England.
B: To whom are you referring?
A: That man behind the flag.
B: How many times did you refer to him?

Referring to someone several times during the course of a speech would be a rather different sort of thing. If I mention a man's name I would not ordinarily be said to have referred to him in so doing. Using a man's name is in some ways opposed to referring to him rather than an instance of it.

If we assume that whenever in an assertion something is mentioned by name by a speaker he is referring to that thing certain very paradoxical conclusions can be deduced. It would follow that when I write in my paper 'I am not, of course, referring to Ludwig Wittgenstein' I would be referring to Ludwig Wittgenstein. But if someone were asked to show where in my paper I had referred to Ludwig Wittgenstein it would be absurd for him to point to the statement in which I say, 'I am not referring to Ludwig Wittgenstein.' The same would be true of the statement in which I say, 'I am referring to Ludwig Wittgenstein.' In both cases I would have used Wittgenstein's name. Therefore, to mention someone by name is not necessarily to refer to him. And consider this example. Suppose the porter at Magdalen College asks me whom I am looking for. I answer, 'Gilbert Ryle.' Would anyone say I had referred to Gilbert Ryle? But if I say, in the course of a talk, 'I am not referring to the most important of present-day philosophers', I would then and there be referring to Ludwig Wittgenstein; though in saying as I just did, 'I would then and there be referring to Ludwig Wittgenstein', I could not be said to have referred to Ludwig Wittgenstein. And this is so notwithstanding the fact that Ludwig Wittgenstein is the most important of present-day philosophers. This, then, is the paradox of reference. In saying 'I am referring to Ludwig Wittgenstein' I am not referring to Ludwig Wittgenstein.[1]

Strawson has argued correctly that if I claim, e.g., 'The king of

---

[1] Philosophical tradition sanctions the production of such paradoxes. I am thinking of Meinong's paradox about objects, of which it is true to say that no such objects exist; and Frege's paradox that the concept horse is not a concept.

France is Charles de Gaulle', what I have said is neither true nor false. The reason for this is not, as he says, that I have failed to refer in saying, 'The king of France . . .' The reason is that France is not a monarchy and there is no king of France. Just so, and said of a spinster, 'Her husband is kind to her' is neither true nor false. But a speaker might very well be referring to someone in using these words, for he may think that someone is the husband of the lady (who in fact is a spinster). Still, the statement is neither true nor false, for it presupposes that the lady has a husband, which she has not. This last refutes Strawson's thesis that if the presupposition of existence is not satisfied the speaker has failed to refer. For here that presupposition is false, but still the speaker has referred to someone, namely, the man mistakenly taken to be her husband.

Of course a man may 'fail to refer', but not as Strawson uses this expression. For example, in your article you may fail to refer to my article.

4. Referring does not have the omnipresence accorded to it in the philosophical literature. It sounds odd to say that when I say 'Santa Claus lives at the North Pole' I am referring to Santa Claus, or that when I say 'The round square does not exist' I am referring to the round square. Must I be referring to something? Philosophers ask, 'How is it possible to refer to something which does not exist?' But often the examples produced in which we are supposed to do this ('Hamlet was a prince of Denmark', 'Pegasus was captured by Bellerophon', 'The golden mountain does not exist') are such that the question 'To whom (what) are you referring?' simply cannot sensibly arise in connection with them. In these cases, anyway, there is nothing to be explained.

How is it possible to make a true statement about a non-existent object? For if a statement is to be about something that thing must exist, otherwise how could the statement mention *it*, or refer to *it*? One cannot refer to, or mention nothing; and if a statement cannot be about nothing it must always be about something. Hence, this ancient line of reasoning concludes, it is not possible to say anything true or false about a non-existent object. It is not even possible to say that it does not exist.

It is this hoary line of argument which, beginning with Plato, has made the topic of referring a problem for philosophers. Still, ancient or not, the reasoning is outrageously bad. Surely here is a case where philosophers really have been seduced and led astray by misleading analogies. I cannot hang a non-existent man. I can only hang a man. To hang a non-existent man is not to do any hanging at all. So by parity of reasoning, to refer to a non-existent man is not to refer at all. Hence, I cannot say anything about a non-existent man. One might as well argue that I cannot hunt for deer in a forest where there are no deer, for that would be to hunt for *nothing*.

It must have been philosophical reflections of this *genre* which prompted Wittgenstein to say in his *Remarks*,

> We pay attention to the expressions we use concerning these things; we do not understand them, however, but misinterpret them. When we do philosophy we are like savages, primitive people, who hear the expressions of civilized men, put a false interpretation on them, and then draw queer conclusions from it.[1]

Let us look a bit closer at what it is to talk about things which do not exist. Of course there are a variety of different cases here. If we stick to the kind of case which has figured prominently in philosophy, however, this variety can be reduced. What we now have to consider are characters in fiction such as Mr. Pickwick; mythological figures such as Pegasus; legendary figures such as Paul Bunyan, make-believe figures like Santa Claus and fairy-tale figures like Snow White. (And why not add comic-strip figures like Pogo?) And do not these characters really exist? Mr. Pickwick really is a character in fiction, Professor Ryle is not. There really is a figure in Greek mythology whose name is 'Pegasus', but none whose name is 'Socrates'; and there really is a comic-strip character named 'Pogo'. In talking about these characters I may say things which are true and I may also say things which are not. If I say, for example, that Pogo is a talking elephant that is just not true. Neither is Pegasus a duck. In talking about these things there is this matter of getting the facts straight. This is a problem for me; it is not a problem for Dickens or for Walt Kelly. What Dickens says about Mr. Pickwick in *The Pickwick Papers* cannot be false, though it can be not true to character; and in the comic strip Walt Kelly does not say anything about his possum Pogo, for Pogo talks for himself. Still, Pogo could say

[1] *Remarks on the Foundations of Mathematics*, Oxford, 1956, p. 39.

something about Walt Kelly (or Charles de Gaulle), and that might not be true.

There is, however, another group of cases discussed by philosophers, and this group has the important characteristic that in talking about its members there is no such thing as getting the facts straight. Here we find Russell's famous example, the present king of France; and Meinong's equally famous example of the golden mountain. What are they supposed to be examples of? Well, just things that do not exist. But in saying this we must keep in mind how different they are from Mr. Pickwick, Santa Claus, Snow White, etc. Keeping this difference in mind, we can see that though it makes perfectly good sense to ask whether Mr. Pickwick ran a bookstore or whether Santa Claus lives at the North Pole; it makes no sense whatever to ask whether the golden mountain is in California. Similarly, though we can ask whether Mr. Pickwick was married or not, *we* cannot sensibly ask whether the present king of France is bald or not.

If the question is 'How can we talk about objects which do not exist?', then it is wrong to use the examples of the golden mountain and the present king of France. These famous philosophical examples, the round square, the golden mountain, are just things we do not talk about (except in telling a story or a fairy tale or something of the kind). Meinong, Russell, and Ryle all puzzle over sentences such as 'The gold mountain is in California', as though one just had to make up one's mind whether to put it in the box with all the other true propositions or into the box with the other false propositions. They fail to see that one would only utter it in the course of telling a story or the like. It does not occur in isolation from some such larger context. If it did so occur, if someone were just to come up to us and say, 'The gold mountain is in California', we would not concern ourselves with truth or falsity, but with this man. What is wrong with him? When the sentence occurs in a fairy tale it would never occur to us to raise the question of its truth. And when we are asked to consider whether it is true or false outside of such a context we can only say that it does not so occur, we just do not say it.

Of course, we may sometimes in error, or by mistake, talk about non-existent things, e.g., Hemingway's autobiography. So here is *one* way in which it can occur that we speak of non-existent objects. As a result of a mistake!

5. It is difficult to read the philosophical literature on these topics (the existence of chimeras, the round square, imaginary objects) without arriving at the conclusion that much of the difficulty surrounding them stems from an insistence that complex questions be given simple, unqualified, and categorical answers. One asks, 'Does Santa Claus live at the North Pole?' The philosopher asks it with the assumption that there must be just one correct answer, for by the law of the excluded middle, either Santa Claus does or he does not live at the North Pole. Russell says that the correct answer to the question is that it is false that Santa Claus lives at the North Pole, for since he does not exist he does not live anywhere. Meinong would say, I suppose, that it is true that Santa Claus lives at the North Pole, for his so-being (*So-sein*) is independent of his being (*Sein*).

But it seems to me obvious that there is no single, categorical, and unqualified answer to our question. Why must there be one? Why are we not allowed first to consider what the person who asked the question wants to know? Surely it is obvious that there are *different* things which may be at issue. Maybe we are dealing with a child who has just heard the Santa Claus story. Perhaps the child believes in Santa Claus and wants more details about him. Then if we say 'Yes, he lives at the North Pole' we encourage the child in his mistaken belief, so from this point of view it is the wrong thing to say. But if the child knows already that Santa Claus is just make-believe, and wants more details about the Santa Claus story, surely it is perfectly correct to say 'Yes, he lives at the North Pole', for that is the way the story goes. A third case is one in which we do not know whether the child believes in Santa Claus and we do not want to encourage him in his belief, if he does believe in Santa Claus. Here we might say, 'No, he does not *really* live at the North Pole. It is just make-believe.'

Now in view of the obvious complexity of the situation, why should philosophers insist that there be single correct answers here? Not only are there different things one may want to know in asking 'Does Santa Claus live at the North Pole?', there are different things that may be at issue when one asks, 'Does Santa Claus exist?', 'Is Mr. Pickwick an imaginary man?' Here are some of the things that one may want to know in asking this last question. One may want to know if Pickwick was a real person or only a character in one of Dickens' novels. One may know that

Pickwick was not a real person, and one may know that he is a character in a novel, but wonder whether he is a real person in the novel or (perhaps) the imaginary friend of a child in the novel. Clearly what is correct to say (or better, what is the least misleading thing to say) depends upon the background in which our question arises. Further, there is nothing, in logic, which requires us to give our answer in one short sentence. Why should we not say something as complicated as this: 'Pickwick is a real person in the novel, he is not the creation of the imagination of anyone in the novel. Of course he is a creation of the imagination of Dickens. He is not a real person at all.' We may *have* to say at least this much in order not to mislead our audience.

In speaking about movies, plays, novels, dreams, legends, superstitions, make-believe, etc., our words may be thought of as occurring within the scope of special 'operators'. Let me explain. Watching the western, I say, 'I thought the sheriff would hang the hero, but he didn't.' The context in which these words are said makes it clear that they are occurring under the 'in-the-movie' operator. I am telling you of my expectations concerning the course of the movie. I thought that a hanging would take place in the movie, not in the cinema. Similarly, I might say, 'Leopold Bloom lived in Dublin.' Is this true or false? Obviously it depends upon whether my words are or are not within the scope of the 'in-the-novel' operator. It depends whether or not I am talking about (say) James Joyce's *Ulysses*. If I am talking about the chief character in Joyce's *Ulysses* and if I mean to tell you that according to Joyce this character lived in Dublin, what I say is true. But if I mean to say that Joyce's fictional character is modelled on a real Dubliner it may not be true. I do not know. But surely what is being said, and what is being asked, is generally apparent in context, and if it is not a few questions can usually make it clear.

There is no doubt that behind these discussions of Pegasus, chimeras, the round square, there is a kind of ontological anxiety produced by certain pictures. One comes across talk of realms of being, of supersensible worlds occupied by shadowy entities not occupying space and time but nevertheless real. Certain images come to mind. Images of things with shapes and sizes, yet not tangible. We think of them as being 'out there' and 'up there', yet nowhere. (It is curious that the picture requires numbers, chimeras, and Santa Claus to be 'up there', not 'down' or even 'level' with us. We picture the numbers standing next to each other like clothes pins on a line. But why should they be 'up there' rather than below our feet?)

It is the influence of such pictures, I believe, which Russell felt when he argued that talk of Hamlet is 'really' talk about Shakespeare. It is difficult even dimly to comprehend what the dispute about whether Pegasus has being, in some sense, can amount to unless one sees the operation of these pictures. One can almost feel the anxiety in this passage from Russell. 'It is argued, e.g., by Meinong, that we can speak about "the golden mountain", "the round square", and so on; we can make true propositions of which these are the subjects; hence they must have some kind of logical being, since otherwise the propositions in which they occur would be meaningless. In such theories, it seems to me, there is a failure of that feeling for reality which ought to be preserved even in the most abstract studies. Logic, I should maintain, must no more admit a unicorn than zoology can; for logic is concerned with the real world just as truly as zoology, though with its more abstract and general features. To say that unicorns have an existence in heraldry, or in literature, or in imagination, is a most pitiful and paltry evasion.' [1]

One wonders just what the issue is between Russell and those against whom these remarks are directed, for surely no one is arguing that Santa Claus is not just make-believe and that Hamlet is not just the creature of Shakespeare's imagination. How, then, does one's 'feeling for reality' enter here at all? I am unable to explain what is at issue except in terms of the 'pictures' I have discussed.

6. It is said to be an astronomical fact of some importance that

(1) The morning star = the evening star.

This was not always known, but the identification was early made by the Greeks. Frege said that it was because the two expressions 'the morning star' and 'the evening star' had the same reference that (1) was true, and because these two had different senses that (1) was not a trivial thing to say.

---

[1] *Introduction to Mathematical Philosophy*, Allen and Unwin, London, 1920, p. 169.

Frege's way of putting the matter seems to invite the objection that the two expressions 'the morning star' and 'the evening star' do not refer to the same thing. For the first refers to the planet Venus when seen in the morning before sunrise. The second phrase refers to the same planet when it appears in the heavens after sunset. Do they refer, then, to the same 'thing'? Is it, as Carnap says,[1] a matter of 'astronomical fact' that they do? One wants to protest that it is a matter of 'linguistic fact' that they do not.

Perhaps Frege's view is better put if we think of the two expressions as names, that is, 'The Morning Star' and 'The Evening Star'. Thus Quine,[2] in repeating Frege's example but adding capital letters, speaks of the expressions 'Evening Star' and 'Morning Star' as names. Quine would say that what the astronomers had discovered was that

(2) The Morning Star = The Evening Star.

This is better, for (1) implies (or presupposes) what (2) does not, that there is only one star in the sky both in the morning and in the evening. Also, a purist might object that it cannot be taken as ground for (1) that Venus is both the morning star and the evening star. Venus is not a star but a planet. It would be wrong to say that what the astronomers discovered was that the morning planet is the evening planet.

(2) is free from these criticisms, but still the same protest is in order as was made against (1). The name 'The Morning Star' does not refer *simpliciter* to the planet Venus. It does not refer to the planet in the way in which the demonstrative 'that' might be used to refer to the planet on some occasion. The names 'The Morning Star' and 'The Evening Star' are not that sort of 'referring expression'.

It would be incorrect for me to say to my son as he awakens, 'Look to the place where the sun is rising and you will see The Evening Star', for that is not what the star is called when seen in the east before sunrise. Again, the proposal that we stay up until we see The Evening Star is quite a different proposal from the proposal that we stay up until we see The Morning Star. In

[1] *Meaning and Necessity*, Chicago, 1947, p. 119.
[2] *From a Logical Point of View*, Cambridge, Mass., 1953, p. 21.

dealing with failures of substitutivity in some ways like these, Frege developed his concept of 'oblique' (*ungerade*) discourse, and Quine has talked about 'referential opacity'. Names in oblique contexts, according to Frege, do not have their 'ordinary' referents but an oblique referent which is the same as their ordinary sense. But it would be absurd to suggest that when I tell my boy that if he looks to the East on arising he will see The Evening Star I am not referring to a planet but to a 'sense', whatever that might be. Using Quine's notion of referential opacity, one might suggest that the reason why the proposal to wait up until we see The Evening Star is a different proposal from the proposal to wait up until we see The Morning Star is that here the context is referentially opaque, so that the two names in these contexts do not refer to anything at all. But surely this result is too paradoxical to be taken seriously, and in any case no one has yet told us how to understand the view that a proposal can be referentially opaque.

Under the entry for 'Venus' in the *Encyclopaedia Britannica* we are given the following information: 'When seen in the western sky in the evenings, i.e., as its eastern elongations, it was called by the ancients "Hesperus", and when visible in the mornings, i.e., at its western elongations, "Phosphorus".' Did the astronomers then discover that

(3) Hesperus = Phosphorus?

In the entry under 'Hesperus' in Smith's *Smaller Classical Dictionary* we read, 'Hesperus, the evening star, son of Astraeus and Eos, of Cephalus and Eos, or of Atlas.' From this, together with (3), we are able to get by Leibniz's Law

(4) Phosphorus is the evening star.

And avoiding unnecessary complications, let us interpret this as meaning

(5) Phosphorus is The Evening Star.

Any competent classicist knows that this is not true.

Under the entry on 'Phosphorus' in Smith's *Smaller Classical Dictionary* we find: 'Lucifer or Phosphorus ("bringer of light"), is the name of the planet Venus, when seen in the morning before sunrise. The same planet was called Hesperus, Vespergo, Vesper,

Noctifer, or Nocturnus, when it appeared in the heavens after sunset. Lucifer as a personification is called a son of Astraeus and Aurora or Eos; of Cephalus and Aurora, or of Atlas.' So the stars were personified, and it seems to be a matter of mythology that

(6) Hesperus is not Phosphorus.

Then did the astronomers discover that the mythologists were wrong?

Of course (3) is false, and no astronomical research could have established it. What could we make of the contention that the Greeks mistakenly believed that Hesperus was not Phosphorus? According to the *Encyclopaedia Britannica* (s.v., 'Hesperus'): '. . . the two stars were early identified by the Greeks.' But once the identification was made, what was left to be mistaken about here?

Could not one mistake The Evening Star for The Morning Star? Certainly one could. This would involve mistaking evening for morning. One could do this. In the morning it is just getting light, and in the evening it is just getting dark. Imagine someone awaking from a sleep induced by a soporific. 'But there aren't *two* stars, so how *could* one be mistaken for the other?'

Hence, though it is sometimes made to look as though the Greeks were victims of a mistaken astronomical belief, this is not so. And Quine suggests that the true situation was '. . . probably first established by some observant Babylonian'. If that is the case, a knowing Greek would not have said

(7) The Morning Star is not The Evening Star.

unless, of course, he were in the process of teaching his child the *use* of these words. And, drawing on his unwillingness to say (7) (except in special circumstances when he might want to say just that), we might push him into saying that The Morning Star is The Evening Star, and even that Hesperus is Phosphorus, though now he would begin to feel that these sayings were queer.

The moral is that if we allow ourselves no more apparatus than the apparatus of proper names and descriptions, sense and reference, and the expression '$x = y$' we just cannot give an undistorted account of what the astronomers discovered, or about Hesperus and Phosphorus. Only the logician's interest in formulas of the kind '$x = y$' could lead him to construct such sentences as 'The Morning Star = The Evening Star' or 'Hesperus = Phosphorus'. Astronomers and mythologists don't put it that way.[1]

---

[1] An earlier version of this chapter, with the exception of Part 5, has been published previously as Chapter 5 of Charles E. Caton's anthology, *Philosophy and Ordinary Language*, University of Illinois Press, Urbana, 1963.

# BIBLIOGRAPHY

BUTLER, R. J. 'The Logical Scaffolding of Russell's Theory of Descriptions', *Philosophical Review*, 1954.

CARNAP, RUDOLPH. *Meaning and Necessity*, University of Chicago Press, Chicago, 1947.

CARTWRIGHT, R. L. 'Negative Existentials', *Journal of Philosophy*, 1960. Reprinted in Caton.

CATON, C. E. (ed.). *Philosophy and Ordinary Language*, University of Illinois Press, Urbana, 1963.

CATON, C. E. 'Strawson on Referring', *Mind*, 1959.

CHURCH, ALONZO. 'A Formulation of the Logic of Sense and Denotation', in Paul Henle, H. M. Kallen, and S. K. Langer (eds.). *Structure, Method and Meaning*, Liberal Arts Press, New York, 1951.

CHURCH, ALONZO, 'Carnap's Analysis of Statements of Assertion and Belief', *Analysis*, 1950.

CHURCH, ALONZO, 'The Need for Abstract Entities in Semantic Analysis', reprinted in *The Structure of Language*, edited by J. Katz and J. Fodor, Prentice Hall, New Jersey, 1964.

COHEN, JONATHAN. *The Diversity of Meaning*, Methuen and Co., London, 1962.

FEIGL, HERBERT, and WILFRID SELLARS (eds.). *Readings in Philosophical Analysis*. Appleton–Century–Crofts, New York, 1949.

FINDLAY, J. N. *Meinong's Theory of Objects and Values*, Oxford University Press, Oxford, 1963, Second Edition.

FITCH, F. B. 'The Problem of the Morning Star and the Evening Star', *Philosophy of Science*, 1949.

FLEW, A. G. N. *Essays in Conceptual Analysis*, Macmillan, London, 1956.

FREGE, GOTTLOB. *Philosophical Writings* (Peter Geach and Max Black, eds.), Blackwells, Oxford, 1952.

FREGE, GOTTLOB. 'Ueber Sinn und Bedeutung', *Zeitschrift fur Philosophie und philosophische Kritik*, 100 (1892), pp. 25–50. English translation ('On Sense and Reference') in Frege, *Philosophical Writings*.

FREGE, GOTTLOB. 'The Thought', translated by A. M. and Marcelle Quinton in *Mind*, 1956.

GEACH, P. T. 'Russell's Theory of Descriptions', *Analysis*, 1950.

GEACH, P. T. *Reference and Generality*, Cornell University Press, Ithaca, 1962.

HICKS, G. DAWES. 'The Philosophical Researches of Meinong', *Mind*, 1922.

JACKSON, R. 'Critical Notice of *Meinong's Theory of Objects*', by J. N. Findlay, *Mind*, 1934.

LINSKY, LEONARD. 'Description and the Antinomy of the Name-Relation', *Mind*, 1952.

LINSKY, LEONARD. *Semantics and the Philosophy of Language*, University of Illinois Press, Urbana, 1952.

LINSKY, LEONARD. 'Reference and Referents', in Caton.

LINSKY, LEONARD. 'Substitutivity and Descriptions', *Journal of Philosophy*, 1966.

MEINONG, ALEXIUS. 'The Theory of Objects', Translation in *Realism and the Background of Phenomenology* (ed.), by Roderick Chisholm, Free Press, Glencoe, 1960.

MICHAELIS, ANNE L. 'The Conception of Possibility in Meinong's "Gegenstandstheorie"', *Philosophy and Phenomenological Research*, 1942.

MOORE, G. E. *Some Main Problems of Philosophy*, Allen and Unwin, London, 1953. These lectures were given in 1910–11.

MOORE, G. E. 'Russell's Theory of Descriptions', in *The Philosophy of Bertrand Russell* (ed. P. A. Schillp), Northwestern Univ. Press, Evanston, 1944.

MOORE, G. E. 'The Nature of Judgment', *Mind*, 1899.

QUINE, W. V. O. *Word and Object*, Wiley and Sons, New York, 1960.

QUINE, W. V. O. *From a Logical Point of View*, Harvard Univ. Press, Cambridge, 1951.

QUINE, W. V. O. *Mathematical Logic*, Harvard Univ. Press, Cambridge, Second Edition, 1951.

QUINE, W. V. O. *The Ways of Paradox*, Random House, New York, 1966.

REEVES, J. W. 'The Origin and Consequences of the Theory of Descriptions', *Proceedings of the Aristotelian Society*, 1933–34.

RUSSELL, BERTRAND. *Logic and Knowledge*, Allen and Unwin, London, 1958.

RUSSELL, BERTRAND. *The Problems of Philosophy*, Oxford University Press, Oxford, 1912.

RUSSELL, BERTRAND. *Mysticism and Logic*. Longmans, Green and Co., London, 1925. The essays date from 1901–14.

RUSSELL, BERTRAND. 'Meinong's Theory of Complexes and Assumptions', *Mind*, in three instalments, 1904.

RUSSELL, BERTRAND. *The Principles of Mathematics*, Allen and Unwin, London, 1903.

RUSSELL, BERTRAND. 'The Philosophy of Logical Atomism', reprinted in *Logic and Knowledge*.

RUSSELL, BERTRAND and A. N. WHITEHEAD. *Principia Mathematica*, Vol. I, Cambridge Univ. Press, Cambridge, first edition 1910, second edition, 1925.

RUSSELL, BERTRAND. 'Mr. Strawson on Referring', *Mind*, 1957.

RUSSELL, BERTRAND. *Introduction to Mathematical Philosophy*, Allen and Unwin, London, 1920. Chapter XVI, 'Descriptions', reprinted in Linsky.

RUSSELL, BERTRAND. 'On Denoting', *Mind*, 1905, reprinted in Logic and Knowledge, and in Feigl and Sellars.

RYLE, GILBERT. 'Systematically Misleading Expressions', reprinted in *Essays in Logic and Language*, edited by A. G. N. Flew, Blackwells, Oxford, 1950.

RYLE, GILBERT. 'The Theory of Meaning', reprinted in Caton.

SELLARS, W. F. 'Presupposing', *Philosophical Review*, 1954.

SEARLE, J. R. 'Russell's Objections to Frege's Theory of Sense and Reference', *Analysis*, 1958.

SEARLE, J. R. 'Proper Names', reprinted in Caton.

SHWAYDER, D. S. *Modes of Referring and the Problem of Universals*, Univ. of California Publications in Philosophy, Berkeley, 1961.

SMULLYAN, A. F. 'Modality and Description', *Journal of Symbolic Logic*, 1948.

STRAWSON, P. F. *Introduction to Logical Theory*, Methuen, London, 1952.

STRAWSON, P. F. 'On Referring', *Mind*, 1950, reprinted in Flew and in Caton.

STRAWSON, P. F. 'A Reply to Mr. Sellars', *Philosophical Review*, 1954.

STRAWSON, P. F. *Individuals*, Methuen, London, 1959.

URMSON, J. O. *Philosophical Analysis*, Oxford Univ. Press, Oxford, 1956.

WITTGENSTEIN, L. *Remarks on the Foundations of Mathematics*, Blackwells, Oxford, 1956.

WITTGENSTEIN, L. *Philosophical Investigations*, Blackwells, Oxford, 1953.

# INDEX